Contents

Page

2	Number
4	Measurement
6	Fractions
8	Number
10	Shape
12	Measurement
14	Fractions
16	Number
18	Area
20	Time
22	Fractions
24	Graphs
26	Fractions
28	Measurement
30	Area
32	Number
34	Angles
36	Number
38	Measurement
40	Number
42	Fractions
44	Measurement
46	Angles
48	Graphs
50	Measurement
52	Investigations
58	More practice
64	Assessment

Page

66	N
68	Time
70	Measurement
72	Number
74	Fractions
76	Time
78	Measurement
80	Number
82	Shape
86	Volume
88	Fractions
90	Decimals
92	Measurement
94	Shape
96	Number
98	Area
102	Volume
104	Graphs
106	Decimals
108	Measurement
110	Number
112	Graphs
114	Angles
116	Investigations
122	More practice
126	Assessment
128	Glossary

Number

Add 10 to each of these numbers.

1. 196	2. 2098	3. 4097	4. 6995	5. 9990
6. 8650	7. 4127	8. 3546	9. 7013	10. 5492

Add 100 to each of these numbers.

11. 947	12. 3942	13. 9496	14. 1005	15. 8900
16. 2831	17. 9460	18. 3504	19. 2796	20. 6042

Subtract 10 from each of these numbers.

21. 105	22. 2903	23. 1905	24. 9003	25. 8007

Now do these:

26.
$$\begin{array}{r} 248 \\ 69 \\ + 1305 \\ \hline \end{array}$$

27.
$$\begin{array}{r} 1629 \\ 408 \\ + 3393 \\ \hline \end{array}$$

28.
$$\begin{array}{r} 36 \\ 2948 \\ + 1072 \\ \hline \end{array}$$

29.
$$\begin{array}{r} 4078 \\ 1972 \\ + 2869 \\ \hline \end{array}$$

30.
$$\begin{array}{r} 672 \\ 4308 \\ + 1546 \\ \hline \end{array}$$

31.
$$\begin{array}{r} 3624 \\ - 1373 \\ \hline \end{array}$$

32.
$$\begin{array}{r} 4062 \\ - 1939 \\ \hline \end{array}$$

33.
$$\begin{array}{r} 4217 \\ - 1938 \\ \hline \end{array}$$

34.
$$\begin{array}{r} 5000 \\ - 1729 \\ \hline \end{array}$$

35.
$$\begin{array}{r} 6312 \\ - 1993 \\ \hline \end{array}$$

36.
$$\begin{array}{r} 214 \\ \times \quad 4 \\ \hline \end{array}$$

37.
$$\begin{array}{r} 1605 \\ \times \quad 6 \\ \hline \end{array}$$

38.
$$\begin{array}{r} 1877 \\ \times \quad 3 \\ \hline \end{array}$$

39.
$$\begin{array}{r} 1075 \\ \times \quad 9 \\ \hline \end{array}$$

40.
$$\begin{array}{r} 1143 \\ \times \quad 8 \\ \hline \end{array}$$

41. $4\overline{)4624}$

42. $7\overline{)3836}$

43. $5\overline{)7005}$

44. $8\overline{)9432}$

45. $10\overline{)6420}$

46. $9\overline{)6318}$

47. $2\overline{)1372}$

48. $6\overline{)4452}$

1. Find the total of 2613, 108 and 1093.

2. Find the difference between 407 and 1303.

3. By how much is 1450 greater than 975?

4. Add together 4370, 36 and 949.

5. Which number is 3 times greater than 1784?

6. Find the number which is 6 times as large as 780.

7. Which number is $\frac{1}{4}$ of 5624?

8. Divide 7364 into 7 equal groups.

9. £
  4·62
  3·48
+ 0·79

10. £
  8·64
  2·49
+ 3·70

11. £
  5·04
  0·93
+ 2·87

12. £
  4·89
  1·95
+ 2·62

13. £
  3·07
  7·69
+ 2·82

14. £
  6·38
− 4·26

15. £
  3·86
− 1·79

16. £
  5·24
− 3·78

17. £
  4·03
− 2·26

18. £
  7·51
− 5·62

19. £
  3·28
×   7

20. £
  4·09
×   6

21. £
  5·56
×   8

22. £
  7·45
×   10

23. £
  4·27
×   9

24. £
5⟌6·45

25. £
4⟌3·76

26. £
8⟌12·56

27. £
9⟌22·41

Measurement

What are the readings shown?

1.

2.

3.

4.

5.

6.

7.

8.

9.

10.

11.

Spring-balance, scales, bathroom scales

Find 6 things to weigh using a spring-balance.
Estimate the weight of each object.
Weigh each object.
Record your results in a table.

Object	Estimate	Weight

Now find 6 things to weigh using scales.
Estimate the weight of each object.
Weigh each object.
Record your results in a table.

Object	Estimate	Weight

Estimate the weight of 6 friends.
Weigh them.
Record your results in a table.

Name	Estimate	Weight

Fractions

4 equal parts.
Each part is $\frac{1}{4}$.

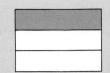
3 equal parts.
Each part is $\frac{1}{3}$.

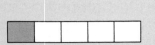
5 equal parts.
Each part is $\frac{1}{5}$.

Write the fraction shaded.

1.

2.

3.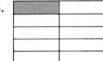

4.

5.

6.

7.

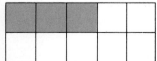
Each part is $\frac{1}{3}$.
Two parts are shaded.
$\frac{2}{3}$ is shaded.

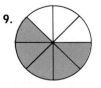
Each part is $\frac{1}{5}$.
Three parts are shaded.
$\frac{3}{5}$ is shaded.

Write the fraction shaded.

8.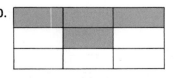

9.

10.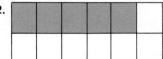

11.

12.

13.

$\frac{1}{2} = \frac{2}{4}$

$\frac{1}{2}$ is the same as $\frac{2}{4}$.

$\frac{1}{2}$ and $\frac{2}{4}$ are **equivalent fractions**.

Equivalent fractions are worth the same.

Complete these:

1. $\frac{2}{3} = \frac{*}{6}$

2. $\frac{3}{4} = \frac{*}{8}$

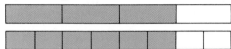

3. $\frac{3}{5} = \frac{*}{10}$

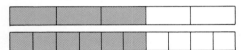

4. $\frac{5}{6} = \frac{*}{12}$

5. $\frac{1}{3} = \frac{*}{9}$

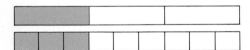

6. $\frac{3}{4} = \frac{*}{12}$

7. $\frac{2}{5} = \frac{*}{10}$

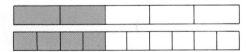

8. $\frac{2}{3} = \frac{*}{9}$

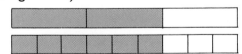

9. $\frac{1}{2} = \frac{*}{6} = \frac{*}{10}$

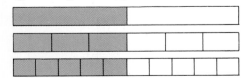

10. $\frac{1}{4} = \frac{*}{8} = \frac{*}{12}$

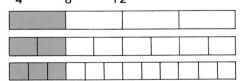

Number

1. Write all the factors of 24.

2. Which number is a factor of both 15 and 20?

3. Write all the numbers up to 28 which have 3 as a factor.

4. Which numbers between 30 and 50 have 7 as a factor?

5. How can you tell quickly which numbers have 10 as a factor?

> When two numbers are multiplied the answer is called the **product**.

Find the product of these numbers.

6. 93 and 7

7. 128 and 9

8. 6 and 143

9. 810 and 10

10. 5 and 964

11. 203 and 8

12. How much would I pay for 3 pairs of socks at 95p a pair?

13. What would 8 potted plants cost at £1.35 each?

14. Ties are £1.99 each. How much would 3 cost?

15. Model aeroplanes cost £2.75 each.
    I have saved £4.80.
    How much more will I need to buy 2 of them?

16. John helps to deliver papers each day, except Sunday.
    The newsagent pays him £1.35 a day.
    How much does he earn in a week?

17. I buy 2 books at £7.75 each.
    How much change will I get from £20?

Mr. Murray is a bookseller.
The prices of his books
are shown in the photograph.

1. Tony bought 2 books of each price.
   How much did he spend at the bookshop?

2. His brother Peter bought 3 books of each price, except the dearest.
   How much did he spend?

3. Their cousin Christine bought 5 books at the dearest price,
   and 4 books at the cheapest price.
   How much did she spend?

4. Her sister Lynne bought 6 books at 75p and 7 books at 80p.
   How much did she spend?

5. Who spent the most money?

6. How much more did Lynne spend than Peter?

7. How much did they spend altogether at the bookshop?

8. Karen has a book token worth £2.50.
   Choose books for her so that she spends exactly £2.50.
   Say how many of each price you chose.

9

Shape

Plain paper, squared paper

Remember: ≫ This means copy into your book.

Fold the plain paper in half.
Draw a shape against the fold.
Cut out the shape.
Open the paper and mark the line of symmetry
with a coloured pencil.
Stick the shape in your book.

≫ The shape has one line of symmetry.

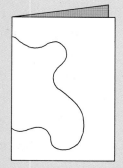

Here is a picture of half a shape.
Copy the half shape.
Draw its reflection to complete the shape.

≫ The shape has one line of symmetry.

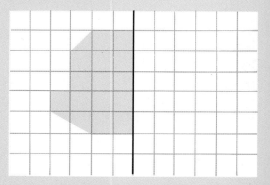

Copy these shapes and draw their reflections.

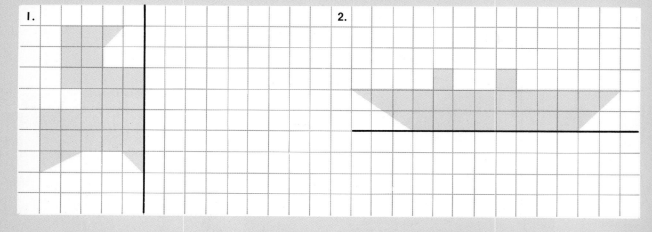

1.

2.

Fold the plain paper in quarters.
Draw a shape against the folds.
Cut out the shape.
Open the paper and mark the lines of symmetry
with a coloured pencil.
Stick the shape in your book.

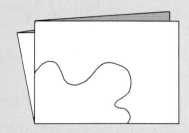

≫ The shape has two lines of symmetry.

Here is a picture of a quarter of a shape.
Copy the quarter shape.
Draw its reflections to complete the shape.

≫ The shape has two lines of symmetry.

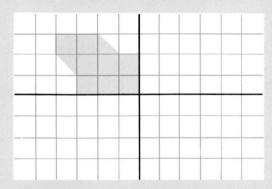

Copy these shapes and draw their reflections.

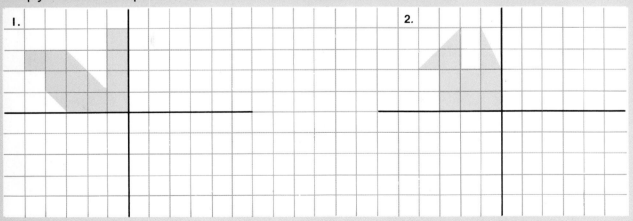

1.

2.

Measurement

Tape measure, squared paper

1. Measure the height of 6 friends.
   Measure their waists.
   Record your results in a table.

Name	Height	Waist

2. Draw a column graph of your results like this:

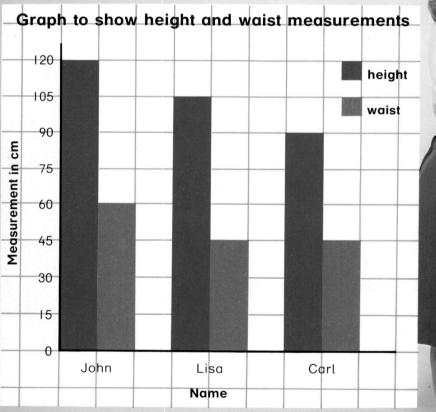

Graph to show height and waist measurements

3. Approximately how many times does each waist measurement fit into the height measurement?

> Hollow 10 cm cube, scales, sand, peas

1. Weigh the hollow 10 cm cube.
   Record its weight.

   Fill the cube with peas and weigh it.
   Record its weight.
   Use your results to find the weight of the peas.

   Fill the cube with sand.
   Find the weight of the sand.

   Fill the cube with water.
   Find the weight of the water.

2. Which weighed the most, the peas, sand or water?

3. What was the difference in weight between the peas and the water?

4. What was the difference in weight between the sand and the water?

5. What was the difference in weight between the sand and the peas?

6. What do you notice about the weight of the water?

Fractions

Complete these:

1.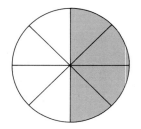

$$\frac{1}{2} = \frac{*}{8}$$

2.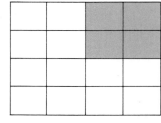

$$\frac{1}{4} = \frac{*}{16}$$

3.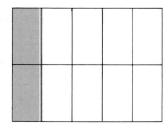

$$\frac{1}{5} = \frac{*}{10}$$

4.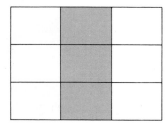

$$\frac{1}{3} = \frac{*}{9}$$

5.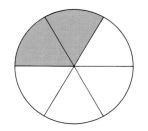

$$\frac{1}{3} = \frac{*}{6}$$

6.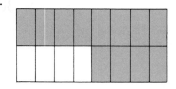

$$\frac{3}{4} = \frac{*}{16}$$

7.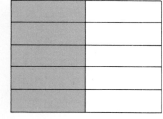

$$\frac{1}{2} = \frac{*}{10}$$

8.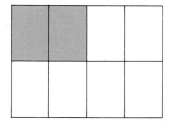

$$\frac{1}{4} = \frac{*}{8}$$

9.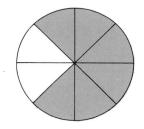

$$\frac{3}{4} = \frac{*}{8}$$

10.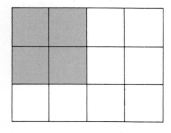

$$\frac{1}{3} = \frac{*}{12}$$

11.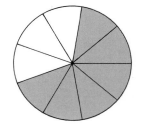

$$\frac{2}{3} = \frac{*}{9}$$

12.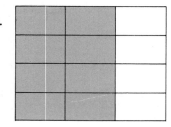

$$\frac{2}{3} = \frac{*}{12}$$

14

To find $\frac{1}{4}$ of a quantity divide by 4.

To find $\frac{1}{5}$ of a quantity divide by 5.

1. $\frac{1}{4}$ of 40
2. $\frac{1}{5}$ of 75
3. $\frac{1}{2}$ of 56
4. $\frac{1}{3}$ of 144

5. $\frac{1}{5}$ of 175
6. $\frac{1}{4}$ of 612 m
7. $\frac{1}{10}$ of £630
8. $\frac{1}{6}$ of 300 g

To find $\frac{3}{5}$ of a quantity → first find $\frac{1}{5}$

then multiply by 3 to find $\frac{3}{5}$.

$\frac{3}{5}$ of 30 → $\frac{1}{5}$ of 30 = 6

$\frac{3}{5}$ of 30 = 18

9. $\frac{3}{5}$ of 45
10. $\frac{2}{5}$ of 90
11. $\frac{4}{5}$ of 75
12. $\frac{2}{5}$ of 100

13. $\frac{4}{5}$ of 65
14. $\frac{3}{5}$ of 105
15. $\frac{2}{5}$ of 85
16. $\frac{3}{5}$ of 30

To find $\frac{3}{4}$ of a quantity → first find $\frac{1}{4}$, then multiply by 3.

17. $\frac{3}{4}$ of £2.36
18. $\frac{3}{4}$ of 192
19. $\frac{3}{4}$ of 500
20. $\frac{3}{4}$ of £7.12

To find $\frac{7}{10}$ of a quantity → first find $\frac{1}{10}$, then multiply by 7.

21. $\frac{7}{10}$ of 1020
22. $\frac{3}{10}$ of 560 m
23. $\frac{9}{10}$ of £81.10
24. $\frac{3}{10}$ of 4020

Now do these:

25. $\frac{3}{4}$ of 236
26. $\frac{2}{3}$ of 564
27. $\frac{3}{8}$ of 328
28. $\frac{5}{6}$ of 414

29. $\frac{5}{8}$ of 760 l
30. $\frac{7}{10}$ of £13.70
31. $\frac{4}{5}$ of 365 m
32. $\frac{2}{3}$ of 405 kg

33. $\frac{7}{8}$ of 640 g
34. $\frac{3}{4}$ of 776 cm
35. $\frac{5}{8}$ of £19.76
36. $\frac{2}{9}$ of 540 m

Number

Set of rails	£12.50 a set
Engines	£15.50 each
Carriages	£2.25 each
Trucks	£1.95 each
Signals	£1.80 each
Station platforms	£2.80 a pair
Bridges	£2.35 each

1. Tony bought a new engine and carriage for his train set. How much did it cost him?

2. Peter bought 2 new carriages and 2 new trucks. How much did he spend?

3. David had 3 new signals and a pair of platforms. How much did he pay?

4. Peter had a new engine and a new bridge. What was the total cost?

5. Alan bought 4 carriages. How much change did he get from a £10 note?

6. Keith added a new set of rails to his train set. He only had £10.75. How much did his father lend him?

7. John had no bridges in his train set. He had £10 to spend. How many bridges could he buy? How much would he have left over?

This is Mr. Simpson's restaurant.
He serves meals at midday and in the evening.
This table shows how many people had a meal at his restaurant during one week.

	Sun	Mon	Tues	Wed	Thurs	Fri	Sat
Midday	84	48	55	73	65	49	32
Evening	79	63	49	84	72	89	94

1. How many midday meals did he serve that week?

2. How many evening meals did he serve?

3. Which was his busiest day?

4. On which day did he serve the fewest meals?

5. How many meals did he serve altogether?

6. Midday meals were £3 each.
   Evening meals were £6 each.
   How much money was collected during the week?

Area

Find the area of these rectangles.

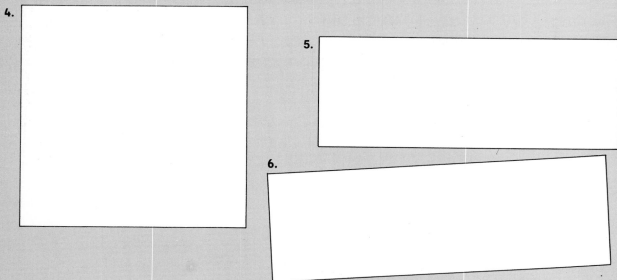

1.

2.

3.

Find a way of calculating the area of the rectangles without counting squares.
squares.
Write how it can be done.

Calculate the area of these rectangles.

4.

5.

6.

Calculate the area of these rectangles.

1.

2.

3.

4.

5.

6.

7.

8.

Time

Look at a current calendar.

1. How many months are there in a year?

2. Write the names of the months that have 31 days.

3. Write the names of the months that have 30 days.

4. Write the name of the month which has 28 or 29 days.

5. How many weeks in a year?

6. How many days in a year?

7. How many Mondays in March?

8. John's birthday is on June 12th.
   Peter's birthday is on July 3rd.
   How many weeks between their birthdays?

9. Sports meetings are held on each Saturday in June, July and August.
   How many sports meetings are held?

10. Susan has to run in the school sports held on August 23rd.
    She wants to train for five weeks before the sports.
    On what date must she start training?

11. Paul is a good sprinter. He will run in his school sports on June 17th.
    The next time he will run will be at the county sports on July 12th.
    How many days are there between the two meetings?

Stop-watch, trundle wheel

Hour hand

Minute hand

This hand measures seconds.

It is called the **second hand**.

The second hand takes **1 minute** to go once round the face.
The second hand takes **60 seconds** to go once round the face.

60 seconds = 1 minute
60 sec = 1 min

Write the number of seconds in:

1. 3 min

2. $1\frac{1}{2}$ min

3. 2 min

4. $2\frac{1}{2}$ min

5. 2 min 15 sec

6. 1 min 40 sec

7. 1 min 25 sec

8. $1\frac{3}{4}$ min

9. Ask your teacher to show you how to use a stop-watch.
Estimate how long it will take you to write this sentence:
"The stop-watch is an instrument for measuring time very accurately."
Now copy the sentence and time yourself.
Write how long it took you.

10. How far can you walk in 10 sec?
Estimate first, then time yourself. Record your result.

11. Now find out how far you can run, hop, skip and jump in 10 sec.
Draw a column graph to show your results.

21

Fractions

Complete these:

1. $\frac{1}{5} = \frac{*}{10}$ 2. $\frac{2}{5} = \frac{*}{10}$

3. $\frac{3}{5} = \frac{*}{10}$ 4. $\frac{4}{5} = \frac{*}{10}$

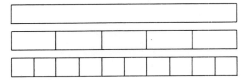

5. $\frac{1}{3} = \frac{*}{6}$ 6. $\frac{1}{3} = \frac{*}{9}$

7. $\frac{2}{3} = \frac{*}{6}$ 8. $\frac{2}{3} = \frac{*}{9}$

9. $\frac{2}{6} = \frac{*}{9}$ 10. $\frac{4}{6} = \frac{*}{9}$

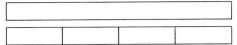
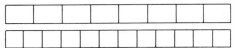

11. $\frac{1}{4} = \frac{*}{12}$ 12. $\frac{1}{4} = \frac{*}{8}$

13. $\frac{3}{4} = \frac{*}{12}$ 14. $\frac{3}{4} = \frac{*}{8}$

15. $\frac{4}{8} = \frac{*}{12}$ 16. $\frac{6}{8} = \frac{*}{12}$

17. $\frac{1}{2} = \frac{*}{8}$ 18. $\frac{1}{2} = \frac{*}{12}$

19. $\frac{2}{8} = \frac{*}{12}$ 20. $\frac{4}{8} = \frac{*}{12}$

21. $\frac{6}{8} = \frac{*}{12}$ 22. $\frac{8}{8} = \frac{*}{12}$

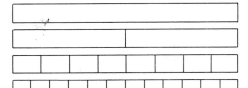

23. $\frac{1}{2} = \frac{*}{6}$ 24. $\frac{3}{6} = \frac{*}{12}$

25. $\frac{1}{6} = \frac{*}{12}$ 26. $\frac{5}{6} = \frac{*}{12}$

27. $\frac{4}{6} = \frac{*}{12}$ 28. $\frac{2}{6} = \frac{*}{12}$

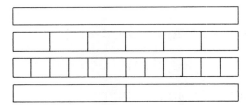

Complete these:

1. $\dfrac{1}{2} = \dfrac{*}{10}$ 2. $\dfrac{3}{8} = \dfrac{*}{16}$ 3. $\dfrac{3}{4} = \dfrac{9}{*}$ 4. $\dfrac{2}{3} = \dfrac{*}{9}$

5. $\dfrac{1}{2} = \dfrac{*}{16}$ 6. $\dfrac{9}{12} = \dfrac{3}{*}$ 7. $\dfrac{8}{10} = \dfrac{4}{*}$ 8. $\dfrac{4}{16} = \dfrac{1}{*}$

9. $\dfrac{10}{20} = \dfrac{1}{*}$ 10. $\dfrac{8}{12} = \dfrac{2}{*}$ 11. $\dfrac{1}{2} = \dfrac{*}{12}$ 12. $\dfrac{1}{3} = \dfrac{*}{9}$

13. $\dfrac{3}{12} = \dfrac{*}{4}$ 14. $\dfrac{6}{8} = \dfrac{3}{*}$ 15. $\dfrac{3}{5} = \dfrac{*}{10}$ 16. $\dfrac{6}{15} = \dfrac{*}{5}$

Complete these by choosing the equivalent fraction.

17. $\quad \dfrac{6}{8}$

$\dfrac{3}{4} = \quad \dfrac{4}{12}$

$\quad \dfrac{8}{12}$

18. $\quad \dfrac{4}{9}$

$\dfrac{1}{2} = \quad \dfrac{5}{10}$

$\quad \dfrac{8}{12}$

19. $\quad \dfrac{3}{12}$

$\dfrac{1}{3} = \quad \dfrac{4}{12}$

$\quad \dfrac{3}{10}$

20. $\quad \dfrac{2}{10}$

$\dfrac{1}{5} = \quad \dfrac{2}{8}$

$\quad \dfrac{4}{16}$

21. $\quad \dfrac{4}{12}$

$\dfrac{1}{4} = \quad \dfrac{5}{10}$

$\quad \dfrac{4}{16}$

22. $\quad \dfrac{6}{9}$

$\dfrac{3}{8} = \quad \dfrac{6}{16}$

$\quad \dfrac{8}{12}$

Complete these:

23. $\dfrac{1}{4} = \dfrac{3}{*} = \dfrac{*}{16} = \dfrac{*}{24}$ 24. $\dfrac{2}{3} = \dfrac{*}{6} = \dfrac{8}{*} = \dfrac{10}{*}$

25. $\dfrac{3}{4} = \dfrac{6}{*} = \dfrac{*}{12} = \dfrac{*}{20}$ 26. $\dfrac{3}{8} = \dfrac{6}{*} = \dfrac{*}{24} = \dfrac{12}{*}$

27. $\dfrac{2}{5} = \dfrac{4}{*} = \dfrac{*}{15} = \dfrac{*}{30}$ 28. $\dfrac{3}{10} = \dfrac{*}{20} = \dfrac{9}{*} = \dfrac{12}{*}$

29. Write 4 fractions equivalent to $\dfrac{1}{3}$.

30. Write 4 fractions equivalent to $\dfrac{1}{10}$.

31. Write 4 fractions equivalent to $\dfrac{3}{5}$.

Graphs

This table shows the depth of some of the seas of the world.

Sea	Approximate depth in m
North Sea	600
Irish Sea	200
Red Sea	1100
Black Sea	2200
English Channel	100

This information can be shown as a graph.

Instead of drawing columns to show the information, straight lines can be used like this.

This graph is called a **stick graph**.
Copy it into your book.

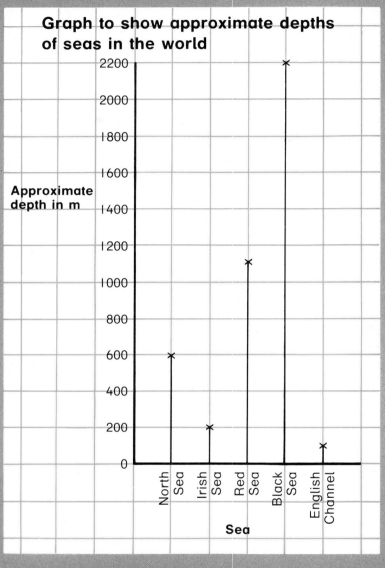

Graph to show approximate depths of seas in the world

24

Bean bag, trundle wheel

Stand at the edge of the playground.
Throw the bean bag as far as you can.
Measure how far you threw it.
Measure to the nearest metre.

Throw the bean bag 5 more times.
Measure the distance you threw it each time.
Make a table of your results like this:

Throw	1st	2nd	3rd	4th	5th	6th
Distance in m						

Show your results on a stick graph.

Draw a stick graph from each of these tables.

This table shows the approximate length of rivers in England.

River	Aire	Humber	Ouse	Severn	Thames	Trent
Length in km	110	70	250	360	340	280

This table shows the approximate height of mountains and hills in Great Britain.

Mountain	Snowdon	Ben Nevis	Kinder Scout	Wrekin	Scafell Pike
Height in m	1100	1300	600	400	1000

Make sure all your graphs have labels.

Fractions

The number under the line in a fraction is called **the denominator.** $\dfrac{1}{3}$

To change $\dfrac{2}{3}$ and $\dfrac{3}{4}$ to the same denominator, they must both be changed to twelfths.

$\dfrac{2}{3}$ is the same as $\dfrac{8}{12}$.

$\dfrac{3}{4}$ is the same as $\dfrac{9}{12}$.

Change these fractions to the same denominators.

1. $\dfrac{2}{3}, \dfrac{1}{2}$
2. $\dfrac{1}{4}, \dfrac{1}{3}$
3. $\dfrac{1}{2}, \dfrac{3}{10}$
4. $\dfrac{3}{5}, \dfrac{2}{3}$

5. $\dfrac{1}{3}, \dfrac{3}{8}$
6. $\dfrac{3}{4}, \dfrac{3}{5}$
7. $\dfrac{5}{6}, \dfrac{3}{4}$
8. $\dfrac{1}{3}, \dfrac{5}{6}$

9. $\dfrac{3}{4}, \dfrac{2}{3}$
10. $\dfrac{5}{12}, \dfrac{3}{8}$
11. $\dfrac{1}{4}, \dfrac{5}{6}$
12. $\dfrac{4}{9}, \dfrac{1}{6}$

13. $\dfrac{3}{4}, \dfrac{7}{8}$
14. $\dfrac{5}{12}, \dfrac{2}{3}$
15. $\dfrac{1}{3}, \dfrac{1}{5}$
16. $\dfrac{7}{12}, \dfrac{3}{4}$

17. $\dfrac{5}{6}, \dfrac{1}{2}$
18. $\dfrac{4}{9}, \dfrac{5}{6}$
19. $\dfrac{3}{8}, \dfrac{2}{3}$
20. $\dfrac{2}{9}, \dfrac{1}{2}$

Put these fractions in order, largest first.
Change them to the same denominator first.

21. $\dfrac{1}{3}, \dfrac{1}{4}, \dfrac{1}{2}$
22. $\dfrac{3}{4}, \dfrac{7}{8}, \dfrac{5}{12}$
23. $\dfrac{1}{6}, \dfrac{1}{4}, \dfrac{5}{12}$
24. $\dfrac{2}{3}, \dfrac{1}{4}, \dfrac{5}{6}$

25. $\dfrac{1}{2}, \dfrac{2}{5}, \dfrac{3}{10}$
26. $\dfrac{5}{6}, \dfrac{2}{3}, \dfrac{7}{12}$
27. $\dfrac{3}{4}, \dfrac{11}{12}, \dfrac{5}{6}$
28. $\dfrac{5}{9}, \dfrac{1}{2}, \dfrac{2}{3}$

29. $\dfrac{7}{8}, \dfrac{3}{4}, \dfrac{2}{3}$
30. $\dfrac{2}{9}, \dfrac{1}{6}, \dfrac{1}{3}$
31. $\dfrac{2}{3}, \dfrac{5}{8}, \dfrac{5}{6}$
32. $\dfrac{5}{6}, \dfrac{7}{10}, \dfrac{4}{5}$

Put these fractions in order, smallest first.

33. $\dfrac{1}{2}, \dfrac{3}{4}, \dfrac{1}{3}$
34. $\dfrac{5}{6}, \dfrac{3}{4}, \dfrac{11}{12}$
35. $\dfrac{3}{4}, \dfrac{2}{3}, \dfrac{5}{8}$
36. $\dfrac{4}{9}, \dfrac{1}{2}, \dfrac{1}{3}$

37. $\dfrac{7}{8}, \dfrac{5}{6}, \dfrac{2}{3}$
38. $\dfrac{3}{5}, \dfrac{7}{10}, \dfrac{2}{3}$
39. $\dfrac{1}{2}, \dfrac{3}{5}, \dfrac{3}{10}$
40. $\dfrac{5}{9}, \dfrac{5}{6}, \dfrac{2}{3}$

To add fractions,
the denominators
must be the same.

$$\frac{1}{3} + \frac{1}{2}$$

$$= \frac{2}{6} + \frac{3}{6}$$

$$= \frac{5}{6}$$

Add these fractions.

1. $\frac{1}{4} + \frac{1}{3}$ 2. $\frac{1}{2} + \frac{3}{10}$ 3. $\frac{2}{5} + \frac{1}{3}$ 4. $\frac{1}{3} + \frac{1}{2}$

5. $\frac{5}{8} + \frac{1}{3}$ 6. $\frac{1}{4} + \frac{3}{5}$ 7. $\frac{1}{5} + \frac{2}{5}$ 8. $\frac{1}{6} + \frac{3}{4}$

9. $\frac{2}{3} + \frac{1}{4}$ 10. $\frac{5}{12} + \frac{1}{3}$ 11. $\frac{1}{10} + \frac{1}{4}$ 12. $\frac{4}{9} + \frac{1}{6}$

13. $\frac{2}{3} + \frac{1}{8}$ 14. $\frac{1}{6} + \frac{1}{4}$ 15. $\frac{1}{6} + \frac{3}{8}$ 16. $\frac{1}{2} + \frac{3}{8}$

17. $\frac{1}{2} + \frac{1}{10}$ 18. $\frac{1}{4} + \frac{3}{8}$ 19. $\frac{1}{12} + \frac{1}{3}$ 20. $\frac{5}{12} + \frac{1}{2}$

21. $\frac{1}{9} + \frac{1}{2}$ 22. $\frac{2}{5} + \frac{1}{4}$ 23. $\frac{1}{9} + \frac{1}{6}$ 24. $\frac{3}{10} + \frac{3}{5}$

25. $\frac{1}{2} + \frac{1}{8}$ 26. $\frac{1}{4} + \frac{3}{10}$ 27. $\frac{1}{3} + \frac{3}{8}$ 28. $\frac{1}{9} + \frac{2}{3}$

29. $\frac{1}{5} + \frac{1}{4}$ 30. $\frac{1}{4} + \frac{5}{12}$ 31. $\frac{2}{3} + \frac{1}{5}$ 32. $\frac{1}{5} + \frac{3}{4}$

33. $\frac{1}{2} + \frac{1}{5}$ 34. $\frac{1}{3} + \frac{1}{5}$ 35. $\frac{1}{4} + \frac{7}{10}$ 36. $\frac{2}{7} + \frac{1}{4}$

37. $\frac{2}{9} + \frac{1}{6}$ 38. $\frac{3}{11} + \frac{1}{2}$ 39. $\frac{7}{12} + \frac{1}{3}$ 40. $\frac{3}{10} + \frac{3}{8}$

Measurement

Remember: 1000 g = 1 kg
1450 g = 1·450 kg

Complete this table.

1.

g	kg
1375	1·375
2030	
	0·750
3445	
	2·125
740	

Put these weights in order of size.
Begin with the smallest.
It may help to write each weight in g.

2. 450 g, $\frac{1}{2}$ kg, 0·405 kg

3. $1\frac{1}{4}$ kg, 1·205 kg, 1025 g

4. 2·705 kg, 2570 g, $2\frac{3}{4}$ kg

5. $\frac{3}{4}$ kg, 800 g, 0·705 kg

Which of these weights is the most sensible?

6.
46 kg
4·600 kg
460 kg

7.
0·200 kg
2 kg
20 kg

8.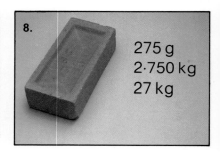
275 g
2·750 kg
27 kg

Write these answers as kg.

9. 437 g + 650 g + 945 g

10. 886 g + 456 g + 538 g

11. 530 g × 4

12. 658 g × 8

Write these answers as g.

13. 1·150 kg − 607 g

14. $1\frac{1}{4}$ kg − 400 g

15. 2·500 kg − $\frac{3}{4}$ kg

16. 2 kg ÷ 4

17. 1 kg ÷ 5

18. 3 kg ÷ 8

19. Decrease 2 kg by 456 g.

20. Double $\frac{3}{4}$ kg.

21. Halve $1\frac{3}{4}$ kg.

22. Find $\frac{1}{5}$ of $1\frac{1}{2}$ kg.

23. Find the total of $\frac{3}{4}$ kg, 875 g and 1·100 kg.

Remember: 1000 ml = 1 l
1240 ml = 1·240 l

Complete this table.

1.

ml	l
950	0·950
1400	
	2·375
2050	
	3·515
4350	

Put these capacities in order of size.
Begin with the largest.
It may help to write each capacity in ml.

2. 705 ml, $\frac{3}{4}$ l, 0.780 l

3. $1\frac{1}{4}$ l, 1215 ml, 1·125 l

4. 2·225 l, $2\frac{1}{2}$ l, 2550 ml

5. $1\frac{3}{4}$ l, 1·800 l, 1650 ml

Which of these capacities is the most sensible?

6.
5 l
500 l
50 l

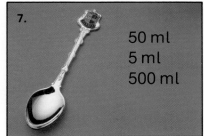

7.
50 ml
5 ml
500 ml

8.
20 ml
2 l
$\frac{1}{2}$ l

Write these answers as l.

9. 546 ml + 395 ml + 857 ml

10. 854 ml + 743 ml + 559 ml

11. 350 ml × 9

12. 466 ml × 5

Write these answers as ml.

13. $2\frac{1}{2}$ l − 680 ml

14. 1·400 l − 530 ml

15. 2·115 l − $1\frac{1}{4}$ l

16. 2 l ÷ 5

17. 3 l ÷ 4

18. 5 l ÷ 8

19. Decrease 3 l by 375 ml.

20. Double $1\frac{3}{4}$ l.

21. Halve $1\frac{1}{4}$ l.

22. Find $\frac{1}{4}$ of 5 l.

23. Find the total of $\frac{3}{4}$ l, 450 ml and 0·875 l.

Area

Find the area of these rectangles.

1.

2.

This shape is made up of the same rectangles as above.

3.

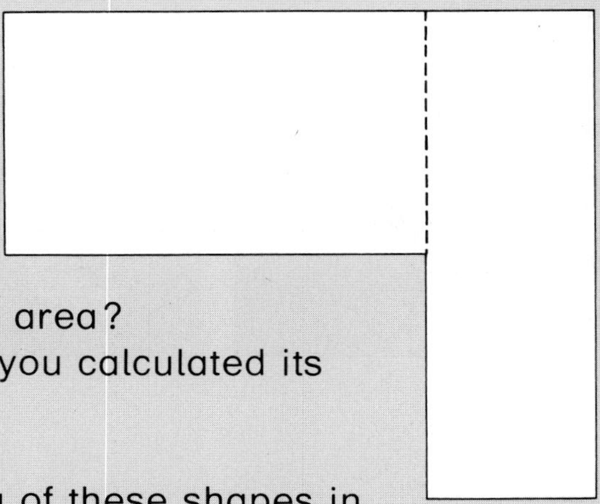

3. What is its area?
Explain how you calculated its
area.

Find the area of these shapes in
the same way.

4.

5.

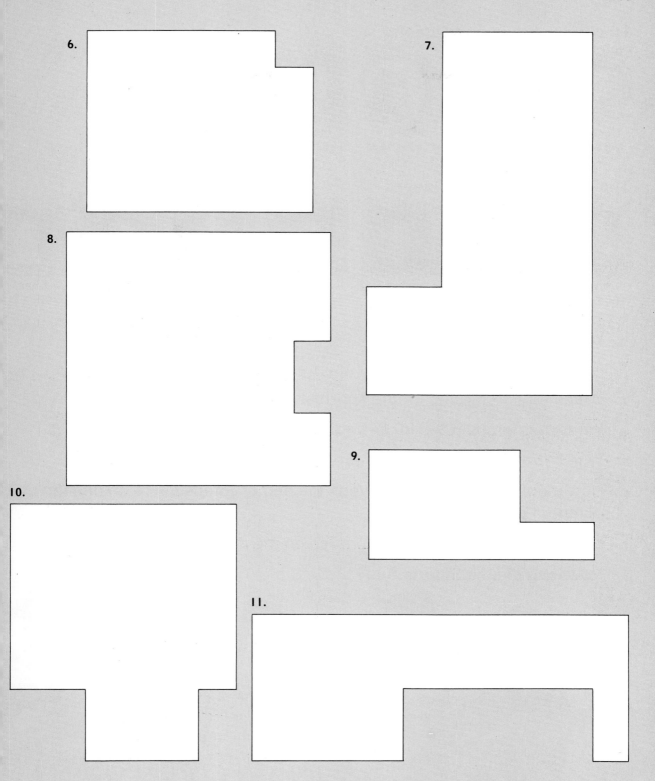

6.

7.

8.

9.

10.

11.

Number

The Tudor Kings and Queens

Henry VII 1485–1509   **Henry VIII** 1509–1547   **Edward VI** 1547–1553   **Mary I** 1553–1558   **Elizabeth I** 1558–1603

The Stuart Kings and Queens

James I 1603–1625   **Charles I** 1625–1649   **Charles II** 1660–1685   **James II** 1685–1688   **William III and Mary** 1688–1702   **Anne** 1702–171▮

1. Which monarch ruled for the longest time?

2. How long did the Tudors rule?

3. Which monarch ruled for the shortest time?

4. Which monarchs ruled for 24 years exactly?

5. Which monarch ruled for 17 years longer than Mary I?

6. How many years passed between the end of James II's reign and the end of Mary I's reign?

7. For how long was there no monarch on the throne?

8. How long did the Stuarts rule?

32

Mr. and Mrs. Severn are moving into a new house.
There are several jobs that need to be done.

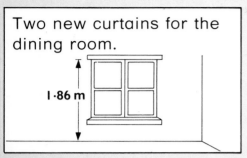

Two new curtains for the dining room.

1·86 m

1. What length of material is needed altogether for the two curtains?

2. The material needed is cut from a piece 4·64 m long. How much material will be left?

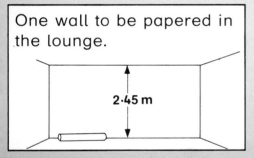

Shelves to be fitted in an alcove.

1·47 m

3. Five shelves are to be fitted. What length of wood is needed?

One wall to be papered in the lounge.

2·45 m

4. A roll of wallpaper is 10 m long. How many lengths can be cut from a roll?

5. How much will be wasted on each roll?

6. Four rolls of paper are needed costing £6.34 a roll. What is the cost of the wallpaper?

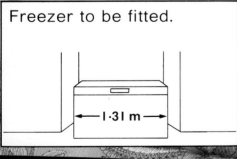

Freezer to be fitted.

1·31 m

7. The freezer has to be fitted into a space of 2·07 m, leaving the same gap each side. What distance will be left each side of the freezer?

33

Angles

Protractor

A **protractor** measures angles.
Here are two types of protractor.

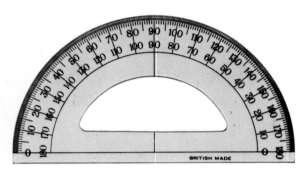

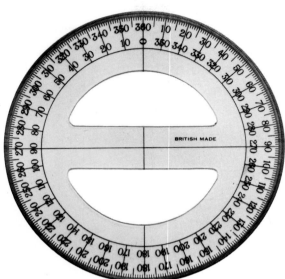

Angles are measured in **degrees**.
There are 90 degrees (90°) in one right angle.

Ask your teacher to show you how to measure these angles.

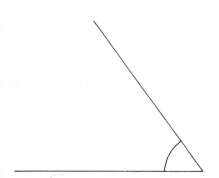

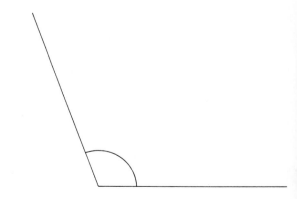

Protractor

Use your protractor to measure these angles.

1.
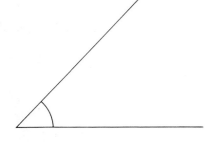

2.
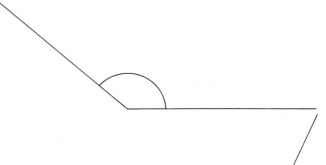

3.
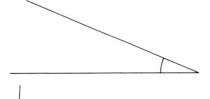

4.
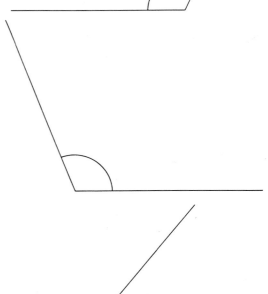

5.
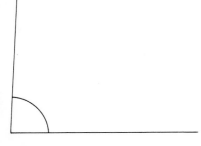

6.

7.

8.

Number

Write the answers only.

1. 264 + 99
2. 306 + 99
3. 514 + 99
4. 185 + 99
5. 462 − 99
6. 308 − 99
7. 947 − 99
8. 838 − 99
9. 164 × 10
10. 138 × 10
11. 200 × 10
12. 946 × 10
13. 230 ÷ 10
14. 140 ÷ 10
15. 389 ÷ 10
16. 473 ÷ 10

Set these out in the easiest way for you.

17. 643 + 27 + 196
18. 749 + 1006 + 9
19. 402 + 1398 + 16
20. 3609 − 416
21. 2906 − 1387
22. 8003 − 3629
23. 1602 × 5
24. 1097 × 4
25. 278 × 9
26. 1175 × 8
27. 6206 ÷ 7
28. 3717 ÷ 3
29. 7256 ÷ 8
30. 9253 ÷ 6

31. John has £1.36.
Jane has 3 times as much.
How much has Jane?

32. Jenny has £8.70 in her
money box.
It is in 10p pieces.
How many coins in her money box?

33. Anne's shoes cost £14.50.
Lynne's shoes cost £11.75.
How much dearer were Anne's shoes?

34. Mother has £10.50 in her purse.
She spends $\frac{1}{3}$ of it on tomato plants.
How much has she left?

Mr. Green has a large garden.
He has 2 greenhouses in his garden.
One is a large one, the other is a small one.
He grows plants in them.
Mr. Green sells his plants at the market.

1. In the large greenhouse he grew tomato plants last year.
   He set them in 8 rows, with 195 plants in each row.
   How many plants did he grow?

2. $\frac{1}{10}$ of his tomato plants were too weak to sell.
   How many plants did he sell?

3. He sold the plants at 2 for £1.
   How much money did he get for them altogether?

4. In the small greenhouse he grew indoor plants in boxes.
   He had 153 boxes, with 8 plants in each box.
   How many indoor plants did he grow?

5. The frost killed $\frac{1}{6}$ of his indoor plants.
   How many were alive after the frost?

6. He sold his indoor plants at 3 for £1.
   How much money did he get for them altogether?

Measurement

1. What is the total of 1·475 kg and 840 g?

2. How much heavier is 4 kg than 2·340 kg?

3. What is $\frac{1}{4}$ of $1\frac{1}{2}$ kg?

4. What is the difference between $1\frac{3}{4}$ kg and 875 g?

5. What is $2\frac{1}{4}$ kg halved?

6. What is 3 kg shared by 8?

7. What must 2 kg be decreased by to leave 940 g?

8. What must 738 g be increased by to give 1·250 kg?

9. What is the total of $1\frac{1}{2}$ kg, 1·750 kg and 875 g?

10. What is the difference between 578 g and 1·364 kg?

11. How much heavier is $2\frac{1}{2}$ kg than 285 g?

12. What is the total of 685 g and 2·521 kg?

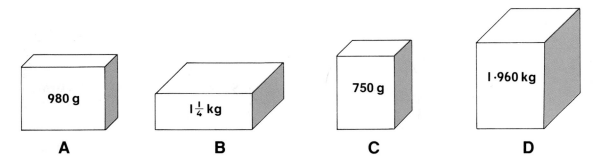

A	B	C	D
980 g	$1\frac{1}{4}$ kg	750 g	1·960 kg

13. What is the total weight of the parcels A, C and D?

14. By how much is parcel B heavier than parcel C?

15. What is the difference in weight between parcels D and A?

16. Which parcel is half as heavy as parcel D?

17. Which two parcels together weigh 1·730 kg?

18. Which two parcels differ in weight by $\frac{1}{2}$ kg?

1. What is the total of 730 ml and 1·750 l?

2. How much more is 3 l than 1·250 l?

3. What is $\frac{1}{5}$ of 3 l?

4. What is the difference between $2\frac{1}{4}$ l and 998 ml?

5. What is $2\frac{1}{4}$ l halved?

6. What is 5 l shared by 4?

7. What must 2 l be decreased by to leave 824 ml?

8. What must 714 ml be increased by to give 1·368 l?

9. What is the total of $2\frac{1}{4}$ l, 1·364 l and 647 ml?

10. What is the difference between 784 ml and 1·638 l?

11. How much more is $3\frac{1}{2}$ l than 620 ml?

12. What is the total of 3 l, 2·160 l and 750 ml?

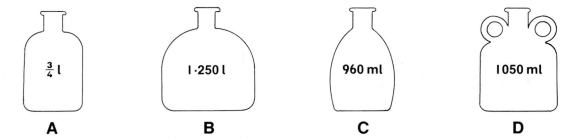

A $\frac{3}{4}$ l   B 1·250 l   C 960 ml   D 1050 ml

13. What is the total capacity of bottles B, C, and D?

14. How much more does bottle B hold than bottle A?

15. Which two bottles together hold 1710 ml?

16. If half bottle A has been used, how much remains?

17. What is the total capacity of 6 bottles of C?

18. Which is the greater, 4 bottles of A or 2 bottles of D?

39

Number

Sometimes it is necessary to count the number of vehicles that use a road each day.
When this is done it is called a traffic census.
This traffic census was taken on a busy road near London.
This table shows how many vehicles were on that road when the census was taken.

	Cars	Vans	Buses	Lorries	Motor cycles
To London	1825	729	136	1001	124
From London	2136	802	172	763	96

1. How many cars were on the road that day?

2. How many lorries were there altogether?

3. How many more cars than lorries were counted?

4. How many more cars were travelling away from London than to London?

5. How many fewer lorries were travelling away from London than to London?

6. How many more cars passed the census point than vans?

7. If $\frac{1}{4}$ of the motor cycles had 2 people on them, how many people riding motor cycles passed the census point?

8. If $\frac{1}{4}$ of the lorries which passed the census point were empty, how many were loaded?

9. How many vehicles were travelling to London on that road that day?

10. How many vehicles were leaving London?

11. Draw a column graph to show the number of each type of vehicle travelling towards London that day.

12. Draw a column graph to show the number of each type of vehicle travelling away from London.

Fractions

Copy and complete.

1. $1 = \frac{*}{2}$

2. $1 = \frac{*}{3}$

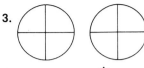

3. $2 = \frac{*}{4}$

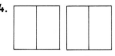

4. $2 = \frac{*}{2}$

5. $3 = \frac{*}{4}$

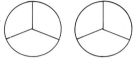

6. $* = \frac{6}{3}$

7. $1\frac{1}{2} = \frac{*}{2}$

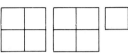

8. $2\frac{1}{4} = \frac{*}{4}$

9. $* = \frac{5}{3}$

10. $1\frac{3}{8} = \frac{*}{8}$

11. $1\frac{3}{4} = \frac{*}{4}$

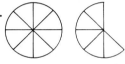

12. $* = \frac{13}{8}$

A number that has whole ones and a fraction is called a **mixed number**. $1\frac{3}{4}$ is a mixed number.

Change these mixed numbers into fractions.

$2\frac{1}{4} = \frac{9}{4}$

13. $1\frac{1}{3}$ 14. $4\frac{1}{2}$ 15. $2\frac{3}{8}$

16. $2\frac{5}{12}$ 17. $1\frac{7}{8}$ 18. $3\frac{2}{3}$ 19. $4\frac{4}{5}$ 20. $3\frac{3}{4}$

Change these fractions into mixed numbers.

$\frac{3}{2} = 1\frac{1}{2}$

21. $\frac{7}{4}$ 22. $\frac{9}{2}$ 23. $\frac{15}{8}$

24. $\frac{7}{5}$ 25. $\frac{8}{3}$ 26. $\frac{21}{10}$ 27. $\frac{7}{6}$ 28. $\frac{19}{8}$

Add these fractions.

Remember to change your answers to mixed numbers.

$\frac{3}{4} + \frac{2}{3}$

$= \frac{9}{12} + \frac{8}{12}$

$= \frac{17}{12}$

$= 1\frac{5}{12}$

1. $\frac{1}{2} + \frac{2}{3}$ 2. $\frac{2}{3} + \frac{3}{5}$ 3. $\frac{9}{10} + \frac{1}{2}$

4. $\frac{5}{6} + \frac{3}{4}$ 5. $\frac{1}{2} + \frac{7}{10}$ 6. $\frac{4}{5} + \frac{3}{4}$

7. $\frac{2}{3} + \frac{7}{8}$ 8. $\frac{1}{6} + \frac{8}{9}$ 9. $\frac{2}{3} + \frac{5}{6}$

10. $\frac{5}{8} + \frac{2}{3}$ 11. $\frac{3}{4} + \frac{2}{3}$ 12. $\frac{7}{8} + \frac{1}{2}$

13. $\frac{9}{10} + \frac{4}{5}$ 14. $\frac{5}{6} + \frac{7}{8}$ 15. $\frac{5}{6} + \frac{5}{9}$

16. This bottle holds 720 ml. It is $\frac{3}{8}$ full.
How much liquid is in the bottle?

17. A full box of apples weighs 12 kg.
What will $\frac{5}{6}$ of this weigh?

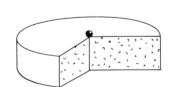

18. A whole cake weighs 450 g.
Jane ate $\frac{2}{5}$ of it. What is the weight of
the cake that is left?

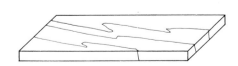

19. This length of wood is 270 cm long. John
wants to cut off $\frac{2}{9}$. What length will be
cut off?

43

Measurement

Here is a picture of a garden.

Here is a **plan** of the garden.

Each cm on the plan stands for 3 m
in the garden.
We say the **scale** of the plan
is 1 cm to 3 m.
or 1 cm : 3 m.

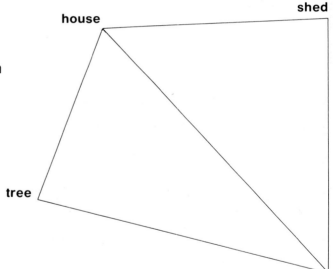

Find the distance in the garden from:

1. the house to the shed;
2. the house to the pond;
3. the house to the tree;
4. the tree to the pond;
5. the house to the tree via the pond;
6. the house to the pond via the shed;
7. the house back to the house via the tree and pond.
8. Find the perimeter of the garden.

44

Here is a street plan.

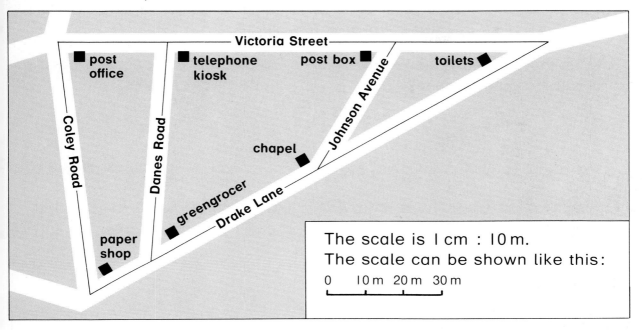

1. How long is Victoria Street?

2. How long is Johnson Avenue?

3. How long is Danes Road?

4. How far is it from the paper shop to the telephone kiosk via Danes Road?

5. How far is it from the post office to the greengrocer via Coley Road?

6. How far is it from the telephone kiosk to the chapel via Johnson Avenue?

7. How far is it from the toilets to the paper shop via the telephone kiosk?

8. How much further is it from the paper shop to the telephone kiosk going via Coley Road than via Danes Road?

9. Describe the shortest route from the post box to the greengrocer.

10. Describe the shortest route from the post office to the chapel.

Angles

Protractor

Different sized angles have different names.

Angles that measure less than 90° are called **acute angles**.

Angles that measure 90° are called **right angles**.

Angles that measure more than 90° but less than 180° are called **obtuse angles**.

Angles that measure 180° are called **straight angles**.

Write the name of each angle, then find out the number of degrees each angle measures.

1.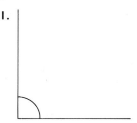

2.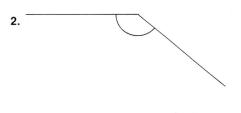

3.

4.

Ask your teacher to show you how to draw an angle.

Draw these angles

1. 60°   2. 85°   3. 32°   4. 115°   5. 162°

6. 17°   7. 48°   8. 144°   9. 27°   10. 95°

Copy and complete this table.

Start at	Move	Degrees	Finish
N	clockwise	90°	E
E	anti-clockwise	135°	
	clockwise	270°	S
SW	clockwise		E
NW	anti-clockwise	315°	
NE	clockwise		SW
SW		270°	NW

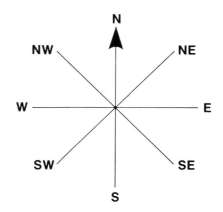

Find the way!

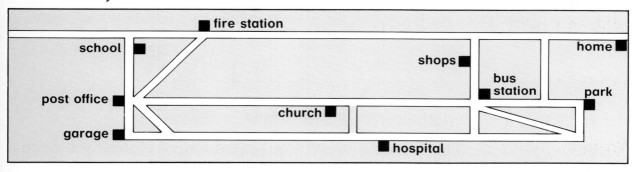

1. Start at home and walk west. What building is on the right-hand side of the street?

2. Start at the post office and walk east. What is the first building on the left you will meet?

3. From home, face due west. Take the first road left and the first road left again. What is ahead of you?

4. Write all the directions you could walk if you stood outside the post office.

5. From the park walk west, take the first road left, going south. Take the next turn right. What building would you see on the left-hand side of the road?

6. Describe how you could get from school to home calling at the post office.

Graphs

The numbers shown on each of these axes are called **co-ordinates**.
Co-ordinates help you to plot points on a graph.
The co-ordinate on the horizontal axis is always written before
the co-ordinate on the vertical axis.

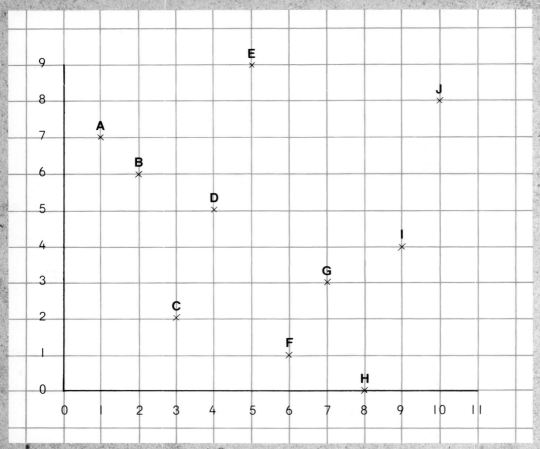

The co-ordinates of Point A are (1,7).
Write the co-ordinates of all the other points.

Draw a horizontal axis labelled 0 to 9.
Draw a vertical axis labelled 0 to 5.
Join up these points in order. (1,4) (2,5) (3,4) (2,3) (1,4)
Now join up these points in order. (3,4) (8,4) (9,3) (9,2) (8,3) (8,0)
(7,0) (7,2) (4,2) (4,0) (3,0) (3,4)

Make up some designs yourself for your friend to plot.

This old map was found in a sailor's chest.
It is a map of a treasure island.
The clues on it explain where the treasure lies buried.
Can you find the treasure?

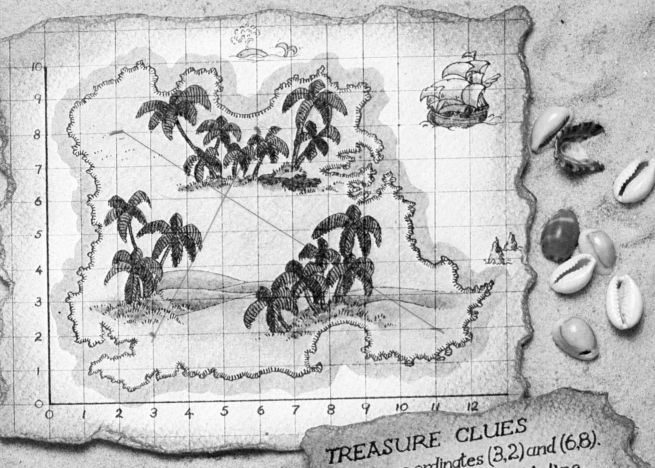

Copy the map on squared paper.
Find the place where
the treasure is hidden.
Write its co-ordinates.

TREASURE CLUES
Plot the co-ordinates (3,2) and (6,8).
Join them with a straight line.
Plot the co-ordinates (2,8) and (11,2).
Join them with a straight line.
The treasure is hidden where
the lines cross.

Measurement

1. $3 \cdot 60 \, m + 5 \cdot 43 \, m$
2. $4\frac{3}{4} \, m + 2 \cdot 87 \, m$
3. $6 \cdot 16 \, m + 37 \, cm$

4. $6 \, m - 3 \cdot 64 \, m$
5. $5\frac{3}{4} \, m - 1 \cdot 86 \, m$
6. $4 \cdot 33 \, m - 2 \cdot 48 \, m$

7. $2 \cdot 91 \, m \times 4$
8. $3\frac{1}{2} \, m \times 7$
9. $6 \cdot 42 \, m \times 9$

10. $1 \cdot 44 \, m \div 3$
11. $22 \, m \div 8$
12. $22\frac{3}{4} \, m \div 5$

When measuring long distances we use kilometres.
A kilometre is 1000 metres.

> 1000 metres = 1 **kilometre**
> 1000 m = 1 **km**

Write how many metres there are in the following:

13. $\frac{1}{2}$ km
14. $1\frac{1}{2}$ km
15. $\frac{1}{4}$ km
16. $\frac{3}{4}$ km
17. $2\frac{1}{4}$ km
18. $1\frac{3}{4}$ km

This map shows the distances between some Italian villages in km.

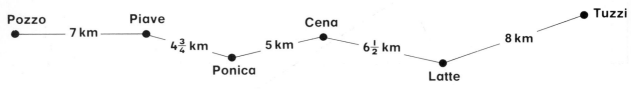

19. Carlo travelled from Piave to Ponica.
    Toni travelled from Latte to Cena.
    How many more metres did Toni travel?

20. Carlo drove from Ponica towards Tuzzi.
    He broke down $\frac{1}{4}$ km before Tuzzi.
    How far had he gone?

21. Toni drives from Cena towards Pozzo.
    He stops for a rest after $10\frac{1}{2}$ km.
    How much further has he to go to reach Pozzo?

Type of aeroplane	One-eleven	Viscount	Concorde	Jumbo jet
Distance which can be travelled in one hour.	866 km	570 km	2400 km	840 km

1. How much further will a Concorde fly than a Viscount in one hour?

2. How far can a One-eleven fly in 3 hours?

3. How far can a Jumbo jet fly in 6 hours?

4. How far can a Concorde fly in $2\frac{1}{2}$ hours?

5. How far can a Viscount fly in $1\frac{1}{2}$ hours?

6. How far can a Jumbo jet fly in 20 minutes?

7. How far can a Viscount fly in 40 minutes?

Investigations

Find as many ways as you can
of scoring 46 with 3 darts.

How would these balls have to
be rearranged so that each line
of three numbers adds up to the
same total?

How would these cards need to
be rearranged so that each line
of three numbers adds up to the
same total?

2 cm squared paper

Draw this on squared paper.

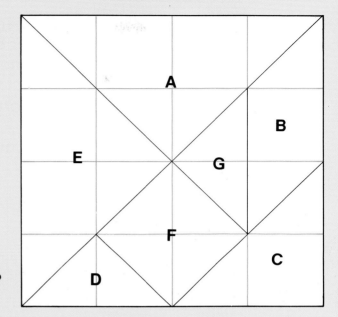

Cut out the 7 shapes.

Which shapes have the same area?
Why is shape B the odd one out?

Use all the shapes, without overlapping,
to make   1. a rectangle.
         2. a triangle.

Use all the pieces to make these shapes.

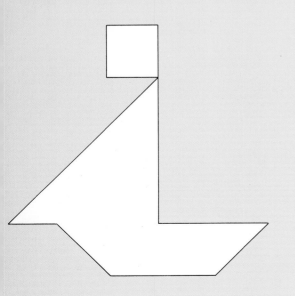

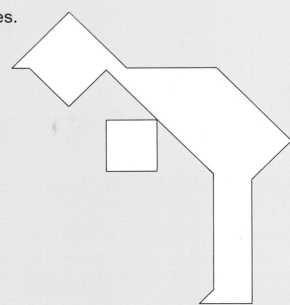

Pegboard, pegs, squared paper

Copy these triangle patterns on the pegboard.
Make the next two patterns in this series.
Write the number of pegs in each pattern.

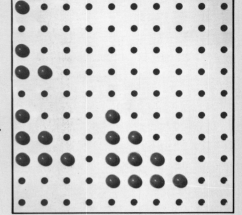

Write the next four numbers in this series.
  1, 3, 6, ...
These numbers are called **triangular numbers**.

Cut these shapes out of squared paper.
Cut the next two shapes out which follow this pattern.

 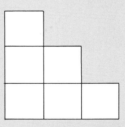 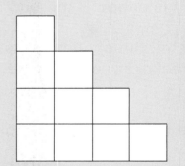

Count the number of squares in each shape.
What are these numbers called?

Arrange the shapes in pairs to make squares.
Stick the completed squares in your book.

What kind of number do you get if you add any
two adjacent triangular numbers?

Write the first six square numbers.
Find the difference between adjacent ones.
What are these numbers called?

Cut out 6 identical hexagons.
Number them like this:

  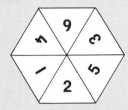

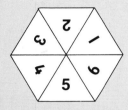 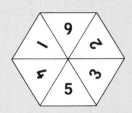 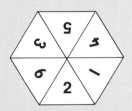

Tessellate the hexagons to make this shape:

Where hexagons touch, the numbers must match.

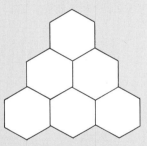

Rearrange the numbers in these hexagons so
that adjacent hexagons have a difference of
at least 3.

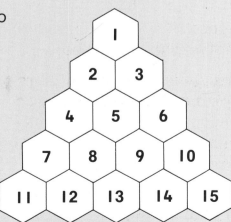

You need a piece of roughly
torn paper.

Fold the paper to make a square
from the fold lines.

Take a new square of paper
and fold it into quarters.

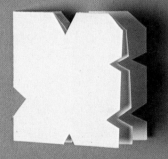

Cut notches out of the sides.
Do not open the paper.

Draw what you think it will
look like when you open it out.
Now open it to see if you
were correct.

Try again with another square of paper.
Cut different notches out of the sides.
Was your drawing more accurate?
How many lines of symmetry has each pattern?

Look for information about Roman numbers in an encyclopaedia.

Marcus

his father

his grandfather

Marcus is XI years old.
His father is XLIV years old.
His grandfather is LXXXVI years old.
Write their ages in our number system.

What do these numbers say?

1.

2.

3.

4.

5.

6.

7.
CHAPTER XLIII

Addition and Subtraction – more practice

1.
```
  3059
   298
+ 1739
_____
```

2.
```
  4131
   269
+ 1583
_____
```

3.
```
   286
  1938
+ 2995
_____
```

4.
```
  1684
  2479
+ 3985
_____
```

5.
```
   395
  4126
+ 1849
_____
```

6. 629 + 3031 + 275

7. 48 + 7209 + 564

8. 3939 + 65 + 1875

9. 416 + 1039 + 5421

10. 2946 + 17 + 1084

11. 3921 + 4653 + 238

12. Find the total of 364, 2926 and 4273.

13. Find a number which is 297 greater than 3929.

14.
```
  4218
 − 796
_____
```

15.
```
  3058
− 1962
_____
```

16.
```
  4630
− 2079
_____
```

17.
```
  5300
− 1876
_____
```

18.
```
  6052
− 2893
_____
```

19. 2964 − 1873

20. 5021 − 3684

21. 6013 − 5876

22. 1628 − 49

23. 2641 − 1938

24. 7000 − 1629

25. Find the difference between 2693 and 1897.

26. Find the difference between 1073 and 3721.

27. Subtract 298 from 1006.

28. How many less than 2000 is 964?

29. From 3706 take 1989.

30. How much greater than 846 is 1350?

31. How many more than 1346 is 1700?

Multiplication and Division – more practice

1. 1428×3

2. 798×8

3. 1037×7

4. 1617×6

5. 792×9

6. 1159×5

7. 807×9

8. 738×10

9. 2492×4

10. 1070×8

11. 738×5
12. 1432×4
13. 786×10
14. 849×6
15. 2939×2
16. 1086×9
17. 963×7
18. 2057×4

19. Multiply 1849 by 5.

20. Find the product of 684 and 6.

21. Which number is 9 times greater than 1036?

22. What is the product of 8 and 523?

23. Which number is double 4864?

24. $10\overline{)4621}$
25. $5\overline{)3575}$
26. $7\overline{)7291}$
27. $3\overline{)2034}$
28. $8\overline{)6237}$
29. $9\overline{)7935}$
30. $6\overline{)5592}$
31. $7\overline{)2808}$

32. Divide 3628 by 4.

33. Find the remainder when 1362 is divided by 7.

34. Divide 3822 into 3 equal groups.

35. Find $\frac{1}{2}$ of 5936.

36. Which number is $\frac{1}{4}$ of 1292?

37. Which number is $\frac{1}{6}$ of 2640?

Money — more practice

1. £
      2·59
    + 3·87
    _____

    _____

2. £
      9·38
    − 2·79
    _____

    _____

3. £
      1·55
    ×   7
    _____

    _____

4. £
    6) 9·54

5. £3·62 + £2·09 + 78p

6. £3·59 − £0·85

7. £4·28 × 8

8. £16·20 ÷ 10

9. £7·36 − £4·62

10. £3·80 + £2·74 + £6·88

11. £5·72 − 96p

12. £2·84 × 9

13. £13·45 ÷ 5

14. £23·67 ÷ 9

15. £6·09 × 9

16. £22·64 ÷ 8

17. Find the total of 79p, £9·68 and £2·73.

18. Find the difference between £6·80 and £2·98.

19. How much more than £3·84 is £6·42?

20. Multiply £7·93 by 6.

21. Share £26·48 equally among 8 people.

22. Find $\frac{3}{4}$ of £7·68.

23. Add $\frac{1}{2}$ of £8·62 to $\frac{1}{4}$ of £9·32.

24. Subtract $\frac{1}{3}$ of £6·21 from $\frac{2}{3}$ of £7·41.

25. How much change will I get from £10 if I buy

    a) a shirt costing £7·99, and a tie costing £1·99?
    b) 4 handkerchiefs costing 65p each?
    c) 6 pairs of socks costing £1·05 a pair?
    d) a jumper costing £8·95?

Fractions – more practice

1. $\frac{2}{3} + \frac{1}{4}$ 2. $\frac{5}{6} + \frac{1}{4}$ 3. $\frac{3}{8} + \frac{1}{2}$ 4. $\frac{3}{5} + \frac{1}{10}$

5. $\frac{7}{10} + \frac{1}{4}$ 6. $\frac{4}{5} + \frac{2}{3}$ 7. $\frac{3}{4} + \frac{3}{10}$ 8. $\frac{7}{8} + \frac{1}{2}$

9. $\frac{7}{12} + \frac{1}{3}$ 10. $\frac{5}{9} + \frac{1}{2}$ 11. $\frac{1}{7} + \frac{1}{2}$ 12. $\frac{3}{5} + \frac{7}{10}$

13. $\frac{11}{12} + \frac{3}{4}$ 14. $\frac{2}{3} + \frac{5}{12}$ 15. $\frac{3}{4} + \frac{2}{3}$ 16. $\frac{6}{7} + \frac{1}{3}$

17. $\frac{7}{9} + \frac{1}{2}$ 18. $\frac{5}{6} + \frac{3}{4}$ 19. $\frac{2}{5} + \frac{2}{3}$ 20. $\frac{7}{12} + \frac{1}{2}$

21. $\frac{9}{10} + \frac{2}{5}$ 22. $\frac{1}{2} + \frac{5}{8}$ 23. $\frac{5}{6} + \frac{11}{12}$ 24. $\frac{3}{4} + \frac{1}{3}$

25. $\frac{7}{10} + \frac{3}{4}$ 26. $\frac{7}{12} + \frac{5}{6}$ 27. $\frac{3}{4} + \frac{2}{5}$ 28. $\frac{5}{6} + \frac{7}{8}$

29. $\frac{3}{8} + \frac{1}{2} + \frac{1}{4}$ 30. $\frac{3}{10} + \frac{1}{5} + \frac{1}{2}$ 31. $\frac{1}{4} + \frac{1}{3} + \frac{5}{12}$

32. $\frac{1}{6} + \frac{2}{3} + \frac{1}{4}$ 33. $\frac{1}{8} + \frac{1}{3} + \frac{1}{2}$ 34. $\frac{7}{10} + \frac{1}{4} + \frac{1}{5}$

35. $\frac{1}{2} + \frac{11}{12} + \frac{5}{6}$ 36. $\frac{5}{12} + \frac{5}{6} + \frac{2}{3}$ 37. $\frac{1}{10} + \frac{3}{5} + \frac{1}{2}$

38. $\frac{7}{8} + \frac{1}{2} + \frac{1}{4}$ 39. $\frac{1}{9} + \frac{1}{2} + \frac{1}{3}$ 40. $\frac{5}{9} + \frac{1}{3} + \frac{1}{2}$

41. Which number is $\frac{1}{8}$ of 2624?

42. How much is $\frac{1}{10}$ of £16·50?

43. What is the value of $\frac{3}{8}$ of £17·92?

44. Add $\frac{1}{10}$ of £14 to $\frac{1}{2}$ of £6·50.

45. Add $\frac{1}{2}$ of 2428 to $\frac{1}{4}$ of 1672.

Measurement – more practice

1.
```
      m
   · 6 · 4 8
  + 2 · 7 3
  _____

  _____
```

2.
```
      m
    5 · 0 8
  + 2 · 9 6
  _____

  _____
```

3.
```
      m
    5 · 2 4
  − 2 · 8 7
  _____

  _____
```

4.
```
      m
    3 · 0 6
  − 0 · 8 7
  _____

  _____
```

5.
```
      m
    4 · 8 3
  − 3 · 0 6
  _____

  _____
```

6.
```
      m
    1 · 6 8
  ×       6
  _____

  _____
```

7.
```
      m
    2 · 0 9
  ×       9
  _____

  _____
```

8.
```
      m
  7 ) 9 · 2 4
```

9.
```
      m
  4 ) 5 · 3 6
```

10. 6·28 m + 64 cm

11. 2·38 m + 74 cm

12. 5·60 m − 93 cm

13. 4·06 m − 69 cm

14. 1·50 m × 7

15. 3·50 m × 8

16. 17·50 m ÷ 5

17. 18·50 m ÷ 10

18. 4·48 m ÷ 7

19. Find the total of 3·50 m, 84 cm and 8 m.

20. How much longer is 2·84 m than 95 cm?

21. Find the difference between 1·50 m and 4·25 m.

22. Multiply 6·50 m by 4.

23. Find $\frac{1}{8}$ of 6 m.

24. What is $\frac{3}{4}$ of 10 m?

25. What will be the total length of 5 pieces of wood, each measuring 1·52 m?

26. Add 2·63 m, 2·82 m and 38 cm.

27. Divide 7·36 m by 4.

28. How much less than 2·46 m is 1·92 m?

29. Add $\frac{1}{2}$ of 1·62 m and $\frac{1}{2}$ of 2·84 m.

30. How much less than 2 m is $\frac{1}{4}$ of 5 m?

Put these in order of size, beginning with the largest.

1. 1 kg, 750 g, 1·500 kg

2. $1\frac{1}{2}$ kg, 1·400 kg, 1600 g

3. $2\frac{1}{2}$ kg, 2050 g, 2·750 kg

4. 770 g, $\frac{3}{4}$ kg, 0·800 kg

5. 1·480 kg, 1500 g, $1\frac{1}{4}$ kg

6. Add $2\frac{1}{2}$ kg and 750 g.

7. Find the difference between 380 g and 1·100 kg.

8. What is the weight of 7 parcels, each weighing 1·500 kg?

9. Divide $1\frac{3}{4}$ kg by 7.

10. Find $\frac{1}{4}$ of 1760 g.

Put these in order of size, beginning with the smallest.

11. 1 ℓ, 400 mℓ, 1·300 ℓ

12. $1\frac{1}{2}$ l, 1450 ml, 1·400 l

13. 3·800 l, $3\frac{3}{4}$ l, 3850 ml

14. 2010 ml, 2·200 l, $2\frac{1}{4}$ ℓ

15. $4\frac{1}{2}$ ℓ, 4·600 ℓ, 4000 mℓ

16. What is the total capacity of 4 bottles, each holding 750 ml?

17. Find the difference between 750 ml and 1·650 l.

18. Add together $3\frac{1}{2}$ l and 650 ml.

19. How much less than $1\frac{3}{4}$ l is 900 ml?

20. Find $\frac{1}{3}$ of 3750 ml.

21. Divide $1\frac{1}{2}$ l by 6.

Assessment

1. 5 2 7 8
     1 0 3 6
    + 9 7 6
    _____

2. £
      40·0 2
    − 1 8·7 6
    _____

3. $1\frac{1}{4}$ kg × 6.

4. Divide 10 l by 4.

5. Find the product of 8 and 137.

6. Find $\frac{5}{6}$ of 2538.

7. Copy this shape and draw its reflections.

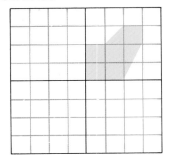

8. Find the area of this shape.

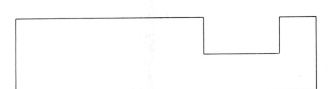

9. $\frac{1}{6} + \frac{2}{3} + \frac{5}{12}$

10. $\frac{3}{8} + \frac{5}{6} + \frac{1}{2}$

11. Change 2 min 40 sec to seconds.

12. Change 135 sec to minutes and seconds.

13. Put these in order, beginning with the smallest.
    a) $1\frac{3}{4}$ kg, 1·705 kg, 1075 g
    b) 2·455 l, 2505 ml, $2\frac{1}{2}$ l

14. Find $\frac{2}{5}$ of 8 kg.

15. Find $\frac{5}{8}$ of £29·20.

16. garage   school

Scale 1 cm : 10 m

library

How far is it from:
a) the school to the garage?
b) the library to the school?

17. Measure these angles.

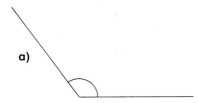

a)

b)

18. Name these points of the compass.

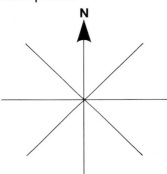

19.
$$3004$$
$$-\ 1729$$
_____

20.
£
$$7\overline{)38 \cdot 43}$$

21. Three bottles each hold 750 ml.
How much do they hold altogether?

22. Which is the heaviest of these weights: $3\frac{1}{2}$ kg, 3450 g, 3·090 kg?

23. Find the difference between 213 and 4002.

24. Write the co-ordinates of each point.

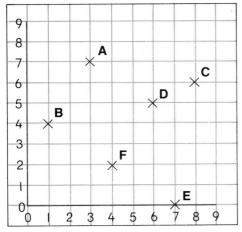

Number

Add 1 to each of these numbers.

1. 409   2. 359   3. 799   4. 989   5. 1999   6. 3099

Subtract 1 from each of these numbers.

7. 320   8. 400   9. 990   10. 4000   11. 6100   12. 7200

Now do these:

13. $437 + 98 + 645$ 14. $7325 + 467 + 739$

15. £7·38 + £6·27 + £4·56   16. £8·37 + £0·96 + £4·56

17. $4076 - 1798$ 18. $7000 - 3421$ 19. £3·08 − £1·29

20. £6·42 − £1·66   21. £4·39 − £2·56   22. 439×10

23. 1576×4 24. £5·26 × 6   25. £7·09 × 7

26. 3926×2 27. 1854×3 28. 2501×4

29. $6 \overline{) 436}$ 30. $5 \overline{) 7965}$ 31. $8 \overline{) 4006}$ 32. $7 \overline{) 5955}$

33. $\begin{array}{c} £ \\ 3 \overline{) 2·76} \end{array}$ 34. $\begin{array}{c} £ \\ 9 \overline{) 14·67} \end{array}$ 35. $\begin{array}{c} £ \\ 7 \overline{) 8·26} \end{array}$ 36. $\begin{array}{c} £ \\ 5 \overline{) 14·35} \end{array}$

37. By how many more is 958 greater than 679?

38. What must be added to 439 to make 1041?

39. Which number when divided by 6 gives an answer of 434?

40. Which number when multiplied by 4 gives an answer of 732?

41. The product of two numbers is 1435. One of the numbers is 5. What is the other number?

42. Add $\frac{1}{2}$ of 1000 to $\frac{1}{4}$ of 2000.

43. From $\frac{1}{4}$ of 360 take $\frac{3}{4}$ of 100.

1. Look at the signs carefully and then complete these squares.

+	20	40	50	70	90	100	110
30							
60							
80							
90							
100							
120							
150							

−	20	30	50	60	90	100	110
120							
130							
150							
160							
180							
200							
210							

Write as figures.

2. Four thousand and nine

3. Six thousand and seventeen

4. One thousand and one

5. One thousand one hundred

6. Two thousand and twenty

7. Five thousand and eighty

Find the difference between:

8. 7213 and 3989.

9. 175 and 1049.

10. £8·74 and £6·85.

11. £0·35 and £2·08.

12. £5·50 and £4·85.

13. £1·50 and £2·37.

Find the total of each of these:

14. $\frac{1}{2}$ of £7·38 and $\frac{1}{4}$ of £5·36.

15. $\frac{1}{3}$ of £9·63 and $\frac{1}{8}$ of £12·64.

16. $\frac{2}{3}$ of £6·03 and $\frac{1}{4}$ of £5·08.

17. $\frac{3}{4}$ of £7·48 and $\frac{3}{8}$ of £11·20.

18. $\frac{1}{2}$ of £5·94 and $\frac{3}{10}$ of £9·50.

19. $\frac{1}{6}$ of £4·44 and $\frac{2}{3}$ of £4·02.

20. $\frac{2}{5}$ of £7·45 and $\frac{1}{4}$ of £3·72.

21. $\frac{5}{8}$ of £7·28 and $\frac{3}{4}$ of £0·76.

Find the product of:

22. 724 and 6.

23. 1293 and 7.

24. 9 and 1084.

25. 8 and 962.

Divide:

26. 3713 by 9.

27. 4049 by 5.

28. 6006 by 3.

29. 7239 by 8.

Time

Is it 8 o'clock in the morning or evening?

So that people catch their buses, trains and aeroplanes on time, all timetables use the **24 hour clock**.

| 8.00 am is written 0800 | 11.00 am is written 1100 |
| 8.00 pm is written 2000 | 11.00 pm is written 2300 |

Write these in 24 hr clock times.

1. 10.00 am
2. 2.00 pm
3. 6.00 am
4. 9.00 pm
5. 6.00 pm
6. 11.00 pm
7. 3.00 am
8. 7.00 pm
9. 1.00 pm
10. 5.00 am

Write these 24 hr clock times using am and pm.

11. 1400
12. 0600
13. 0900
14. 2100
15. 1700
16. 2300
17. 0100
18. 1600
19. 0800
20. 1200

| 9.15 am is written 0915 | 4.35 am is written 0435 |
| 9.15 pm is written 2115 | 4.35 pm is written 1635 |

Write these in 24 hr clock times.

21. 2.40 am
22. 6.20 pm
23. 11.50 am
24. 7.45 pm
25. 3.05 am
26. 10.20 pm
27. 9.40 pm
28. 6.55 am
29. 12.15 pm
30. 11.50 pm

Write these times using am and pm.

1. 1640   2. 0720   3. 0115   4. 2135   5. 1245

6. 0350   7. 2205   8. 1720   9. 1155   10. 1015

11. 0240   12. 1515   13. 1310   14. 0750   15. 2355

16. Copy and complete this table.

half past 6 in the morning	6.30 am	0630
$\frac{1}{4}$ to 4 in the afternoon	3.45 pm	1545
10 to 5 in the afternoon		
		0740
	8.50 pm	
25 to 11 in the morning		
	6.15 pm	
15 minutes past midday		
		1915
	12.05 am	

17. A train leaves Totley at 0710 and arrives at Woolbridge at 1340. How long was the train travelling?

18. An hour and a half after starting from Totley the train arrives at Poolgate. What time did the train arrive at Poolgate?

19. Five minutes later the train travels to Handley. It arrives at 1135. How long did it take the train to travel from Poolgate to Handley?

20. One hour fifty minutes after arriving at Handley, the train arrives at Western Bay. What time did the train arrive at Western Bay?

Measurement

When measuring lines exactly we need a smaller measurement than the centimetre.

This smaller measurement is called a **millimetre**.
10 millimetres = 1 centimetre
10 **mm** = 1 cm

This line measures 8 cm 2 mm.

Measure these lines.

1. _____

2. _____

3. _____

8 cm 2 mm can be written as 8·2 cm or 82 mm.

Measure these lines.
Record your measurements in a table.

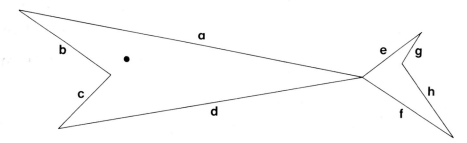

line a	9 cm 3 mm	9·3 cm	93 mm
b			
c			
d			
e			
f			
g			
h			

Cm squared paper

1. Measure these lines.
   Write your answers in mm.

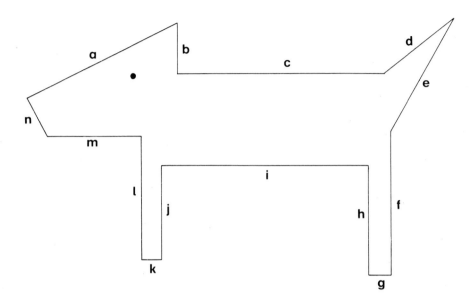

Draw these lines.

2. 84 mm
3. 6·3 cm
4. 9·7 cm
5. 107 mm
6. 119 mm

7. 12·3 cm
8. 7·5 cm
9. 48 mm
10. 51 mm
11. 38 mm

12. On cm squared paper draw a 2 cm square.
    Measure the length of its diagonal in mm.
    Do the same for the other sized squares.
    Record your results in a table.

Size of square	Length of diagonal
2 cm	
3 cm	
4 cm	
6 cm	
8 cm	

Number

This table shows the number of visitors to Beaulieu Museum one week.

Sun	Mon	Tue	Wed	Thur	Fri	Sat
162	120	132	74	102	136	212

1. What was the total number of visitors that week?

2. If the visitors had been spread equally over the week, how many would there have been each day?

    You have found the **average** number of visitors each day.

> To find an average, total the groups
> and then divide by the number of groups.

Find the average of these:

3. 72, 46, 89, 112, 101

4. £15, £9, £8, £12, £6

5. 5 m, 7 m, 12 m, 8 m

6. 12 kg, 6 kg, 15 kg, 9 kg, 3 kg

7. 8ℓ, 5ℓ, 11ℓ, 4ℓ

The following people went to the souvenir shop.

1. Mrs. Mills liked the tea towels.
   She decided to buy 6 of them.
   How much did they cost her?

2. Mrs. Johnson wanted to buy presents for her friends.
   She bought 8 beakers and 6 pens.
   How much did she pay?

3. Mr. Adams owned a café.
   He wanted to buy 90 beakers.
   He was charged a special price of £5·80 for 10.
   How much did he pay?

4. Mrs. Selby bought some souvenirs.
   She bought 4 of each item in the shop.
   How much did she pay?

73

Fractions

Write the fraction shaded.
Write the fraction not shaded.

1. 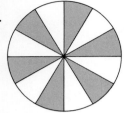   2. 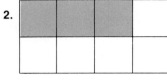   3.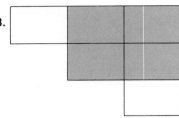

4.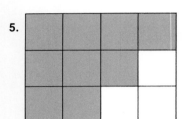

5. 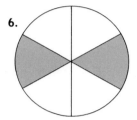   6. 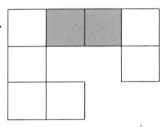   7. (image)

8. (image)

Change these fractions into $\frac{1}{16}$ ths.

9. $\frac{1}{2}$ 10. $\frac{3}{4}$ 11. $\frac{1}{4}$ 12. $\frac{3}{8}$ 13. $\frac{7}{8}$ 14. $\frac{5}{8}$

Change these fractions into $\frac{1}{20}$ ths.

15. $\frac{1}{2}$ 16. $\frac{2}{5}$ 17. $\frac{1}{4}$ 18. $\frac{1}{5}$ 19. $\frac{9}{10}$ 20. $\frac{7}{10}$

Change these fractions into $\frac{1}{12}$ ths.

21. $\frac{1}{4}$ 22. $\frac{1}{2}$ 23. $\frac{3}{4}$ 24. $\frac{1}{3}$ 25. $\frac{2}{3}$ 26. $\frac{1}{6}$

Write an equivalent fraction for each of these:

27. $\frac{10}{12}$ 28. $\frac{6}{8}$ 29. $\frac{4}{6}$ 30. $\frac{4}{8}$ 31. $\frac{3}{6}$ 32. $\frac{4}{10}$

Change these fractions to mixed numbers.

33. $\frac{13}{10}$ 34. $\frac{11}{6}$ 35. $\frac{7}{4}$ 36. $\frac{9}{2}$ 37. $\frac{8}{3}$ 38. $\frac{17}{12}$

74

1. $\frac{5}{6} + \frac{1}{3}$ 2. $\frac{3}{4} + \frac{2}{3}$ 3. $\frac{5}{8} + \frac{5}{6}$ 4. $\frac{1}{2} + \frac{2}{3}$

5. $\frac{7}{8} + \frac{5}{6}$ 6. $\frac{4}{7} + \frac{8}{14}$ 7. $\frac{1}{2} + \frac{9}{10}$ 8. $\frac{4}{6} + \frac{3}{4}$

9. $\frac{1}{3} + \frac{1}{2} + \frac{7}{12}$ 10. $\frac{1}{6} + \frac{2}{3} + \frac{1}{4}$ 11. $\frac{3}{5} + \frac{6}{10} + \frac{1}{5}$

To subtract fractions, the denominators must be the same.

$$\frac{3}{4} - \frac{1}{3}$$
$$= \frac{9}{12} - \frac{4}{12}$$
$$= \frac{5}{12}$$

12. $\frac{1}{2} - \frac{5}{12}$ 13. $\frac{1}{3} - \frac{1}{4}$ 14. $\frac{1}{2} - \frac{3}{10}$ 15. $\frac{2}{5} - \frac{1}{3}$

16. $\frac{1}{2} - \frac{1}{3}$ 17. $\frac{3}{4} - \frac{1}{6}$ 18. $\frac{4}{5} - \frac{3}{10}$ 19. $\frac{7}{8} - \frac{1}{4}$

20. $\frac{3}{4} - \frac{1}{8}$ 21. $\frac{3}{5} - \frac{1}{4}$ 22. $\frac{5}{8} - \frac{1}{3}$ 23. $\frac{5}{6} - \frac{1}{3}$

24. $\frac{11}{12} - \frac{5}{6}$ 25. $\frac{4}{9} - \frac{1}{6}$ 26. $\frac{5}{6} - \frac{1}{8}$ 27. $\frac{3}{4} - \frac{2}{3}$

28. $\frac{9}{10} - \frac{3}{5}$ 29. $\frac{11}{12} - \frac{3}{4}$ 30. $\frac{4}{5} - \frac{1}{3}$ 31. $\frac{1}{4} - \frac{1}{6}$

32. $\frac{7}{10} - \frac{1}{2}$ 33. $\frac{3}{5} - \frac{1}{3}$ 34. $\frac{7}{12} - \frac{1}{2}$ 35. $\frac{9}{10} - \frac{2}{5}$

36. $\frac{5}{8} - \frac{1}{2}$ 37. $\frac{2}{3} - \frac{1}{4}$ 38. $\frac{7}{8} - \frac{1}{3}$ 39. $\frac{5}{9} - \frac{1}{2}$

40. $\frac{5}{6} - \frac{1}{4}$ 41. $\frac{7}{10} - \frac{1}{4}$ 42. $\frac{7}{9} - \frac{2}{3}$ 43. $\frac{4}{5} - \frac{1}{2}$

CHESTERFIELD ● WINGERWORTH   Complete Service   Service 34

Mondays to Saturdays

CHESTERFIELD (EM Bus Stn.)	0620	0645	0655	0715	0735	0745	0755	0835	0850	0855	0910	0935	1021	1035	1051
Langer Lane Terminus	0630	....	0705	....	0745	....	0805	0845	0900	0905	....	0945	....	1045	....
Wingerworth (Lido)	0634	0659	0709	0729	0749	0759	0809	0849	0904	0909	0925	0949	1035	1049	1106
TUPTON (Four Lane Ends)	0637	....	0712	....	0752	....	0812	0852	0907	0912	0928	0952	1038	1052	1109

CHESTERFIELD (EM Bus Stn.)	1105	1135	1205	1221	1235	1321	1335	1351	1405	1435	1505	1521	1535	1621	1635
Langer Lane Terminus	1115	1145	1215	....	1245	....	1345	....	1415	1445	1515	....	1545	....	1645
Wingerworth (Lido)	1119	1149	1219	1235	1249	1335	1349	1406	1419	1449	1519	1535	1549	1635	1649
TUPTON (Four Lane Ends)	....	1152	....	1238	1252	1338	1352	1409	....	1452	....	1538	1552	1638	1652

CHESTERFIELD (EM Bus Stn.)	1652	1701	1715	1735	1745	1805	1835	1908	1935	2008	2108	2205	2235	2305
Langer Lane Terminus	1702	....	....	1745	....	1815	1845	....	1945	....	....	2215	....	2315
Wingerworth (Lido)	1706	1716	1730	1749	1759	1819	1849	1922	1949	2022	2122	2219	2249	2319
TUPTON (Four Lane Ends)	1709	1719	1733	1752	....	....	1852	....	1952	....	....	2222	....	2322

1. How long does it take for a bus to travel from Chesterfield to Tupton?

2. How long does it take for a bus to travel from Chesterfield to Wingerworth?

3. How many minutes does it take a bus to travel from Wingerworth to Tupton?

4. If I catch a bus leaving Langer Lane Terminus at 1645, what time will I arrive at Tupton?

5. Richard is having a birthday party at 4.00 pm. He lives at Wingerworth. Which bus must I catch from Chesterfield to get there in time?

6. What is the time of the last bus from Chesterfield to Tupton?

7. My mother went shopping in Chesterfield.
She arrived at Chesterfield at 2.00 pm, and spent $2\frac{1}{2}$ hrs shopping.
Which bus would she catch home to Wingerworth?

This map shows the bus routes connecting several towns. All buses travelling between the towns travel at an average speed of 30 mph.

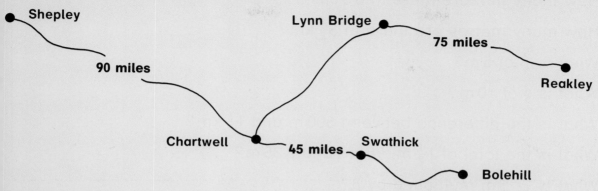

1. The bus from Chartwell to Shepley leaves Chartwell at 0940. What time does it arrive at Shepley?

2. It takes $2\frac{1}{2}$ hrs from Chartwell to Lynn Bridge. How far is it from Chartwell to Lynn Bridge?

3. A non-stop bus to Chartwell leaves Reakley at 0950. What time does it arrive at Chartwell?

4. If it takes $1\frac{1}{2}$ hrs to travel between Swathick and Bolehill, how far is it from Chartwell to Bolehill?

5. How long would it take an express bus (no stops) from Bolehill to Chartwell?

6. An express bus to Chartwell leaves Bolehill at 1830. What time does it arrive at Chartwell?

Measurement

1. How many cm are there in 2·40 m?

2. How many mm are there in 3·6 cm?

3. How many metres are there in $3\frac{1}{2}$ km?

4. What is $\frac{3}{4}$ of 5 m?

5. What is $\frac{2}{5}$ of 10 m?

6. What is the difference between 500 m and $1\frac{1}{4}$ km?

7. What is the total of $1\frac{1}{2}$ m, 98 cm and 2·35 m?

8. What is 2·25 m multiplied by 8?

9. How many grams are there in $\frac{3}{4}$ kg?

10. How many grams are there in $2\frac{1}{4}$ kg?

11. What is 2750 g written as kg?

12. What is $\frac{3}{4}$ of 7 kg?

13. What is $\frac{2}{3}$ of 9 kg?

14. What is the difference between $1\frac{1}{4}$ kg and 1·365 kg?

15. What is the total of $3\frac{1}{2}$ kg, 1437 g and 2·436 kg?

16. What is 946 g doubled?

17. How many ml are there in $1\frac{3}{4}$ l?

18. How many ml are there in $2\frac{1}{2}$ l?

19. What is 1500 ml written as l?

20. What is $\frac{3}{5}$ of 4 l?

21. What is $\frac{3}{4}$ of 5 l?

22. What is the difference between 784 ml and 1·237 l?

23. What is the total of $1\frac{1}{4}$ l, 1·236 l and 957 ml?

Tennis ball, table-tennis ball, golf ball, rubber ball, plastic ball, metre stick

Which is the best bouncer?

Drop a tennis ball from a height of I metre.
How high does it bounce?
It will help if you do this beside a wall.
Repeat it five more times.
Find the average height the ball bounces.

Repeat this activity for the other balls.

Draw a stick graph to show the average height each ball bounces.

Graph to show the average height of bounce

Height of bounce in cm

Type of ball

Number

Mrs. White works at the cash desk in the Globe Cinema. She needs to add up quickly.
To help her, she is making a ready reckoner.

Number of people	Adults	Children
1	£1·65	£1·15
2	£3·30	£2·30
3	£4·95	
4		
5		
6		
7		
8		
9		
10		

Complete the ready reckoner for her in your book.
Ask the teacher to check it.

1. Mr. and Mrs. Wilson and their 2 children are the first to arrive.
   How much will it cost them to go in?

2. Mr. and Mrs. Walters and their 3 daughters are with them.
   How much do they have to pay?

3. Mr. Taylor has brought his 2 daughters and 2 boys from next door.
   How much does he have to pay altogether?

4. A group from the Youth Club are the next to pay. There are 7 adults and 9 children.
   What is the cost for that group?

5. Mr. and Mrs. Benson have 5 children with them.
   How much change will there be from £10?

6. A party of 16 girl guides are next to arrive. Four of them are counted as adults.
   How much will it cost the guides altogether?

7. Mr. Bailey has come to the cinema alone. He gives Mrs. White a £5 note.
   How much change will he get?

8. The school football team are to go to the cinema.
   There are 11 players and 2 reserves.
   How much will it cost them?

Shape

Plane shapes

Find a paper circle.
Make a line of symmetry on your circle.

⫸ Half of a circle is called a _____ .

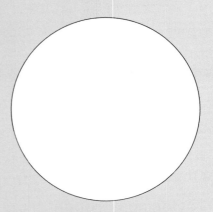

Make six other lines of symmetry.

⫸ Each line of symmetry in a circle is
also a _____ .

Find as many different quadrilaterals as you can.

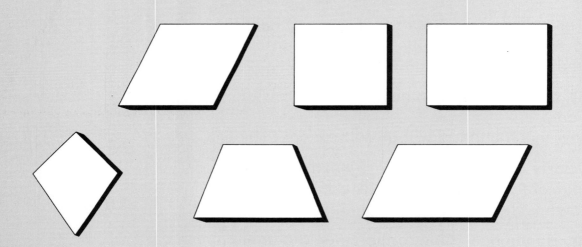

Which quadrilaterals have diagonals which are lines of symmetry?
Draw round them.
Draw the diagonals.

⫸ The diagonals of these shapes are lines of symmetry.

Now draw round the quadrilaterals whose diagonals are not lines
of symmetry.
Draw the diagonals.

⫸ The diagonals of these shapes are not lines of symmetry.

Box of triangles

Draw round each shape on plain paper.
Cut them out.
Fold as many lines of symmetry as you can on each triangle.

Now group your triangles according to the number of lines of symmetry.

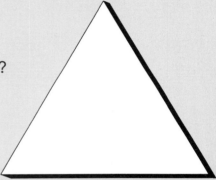

Take a triangle with 3 lines of symmetry.
What do you notice about the lengths of its sides?
It is called an **equilateral triangle**.

Stick all the equilateral triangles in your book.

≫ Equilateral triangles have 3 equal sides.

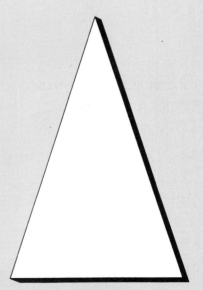

Take a triangle with 1 line of symmetry.
What do you notice about the lengths of its sides?
It is called an **isosceles triangle**.

Stick all the isosceles triangles in your book.

≫ Isosceles triangles have 2 equal sides.

Box of triangles

Take a triangle with no lines of symmetry.
What do you notice about the lengths
of its sides?
It is called a **scalene triangle**.
Find some scalene triangles.
Draw round them.
Stick all the scalene triangles in your book.

≫ Scalene triangles have no equal sides.

Write the names of each of these triangles.

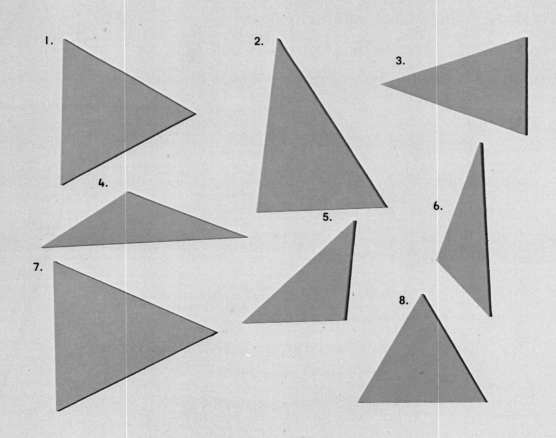

Box of quadrilaterals

Find quadrilaterals which have 4 right angles.
Draw round them.

≫ These quadrilaterals have 4 right angles.

Which of these have right angles?

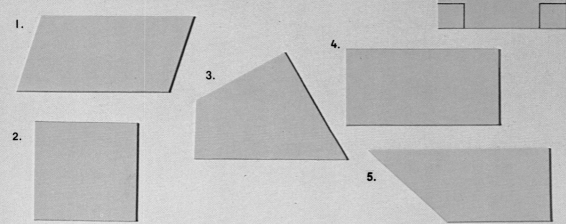

1.
2.
3.
4.
5.

Find quadrilaterals which have lines of symmetry.
Draw round them.
Draw the lines of symmetry.

≫ These quadrilaterals have lines of symmetry.

Which of these have lines of symmetry?

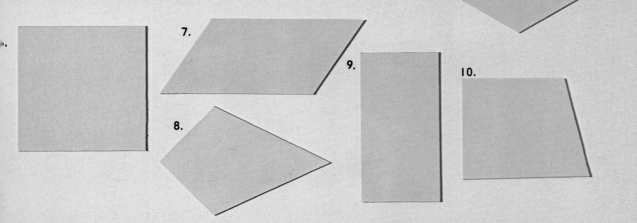

7.
8.
9.
10.

85

Volume

3 small boxes, centimetre cubes

Choose one of the boxes.
Put a layer of cubes in the bottom of the box.

≫ ☐ cm cubes are in one layer.

Find how many layers are needed to fill the box.

≫ There are ☐ layers in the box.

≫ There are ☐ cm cubes in the box.

The number of cm cubes that a box holds is called its **volume**.

Find the volumes of the other two boxes.
Write your answers like this:

Number of cubes in a layer ☐

Number of layers ☐

Volume ☐ cm cubes

The volume of I **cm cube** is written as I **cm³**.

86

Calculate the volumes of these boxes.
Write your answers like this:

Number of cubes in a layer ☐

Number of layers ☐

Volume ☐ cm³

1.

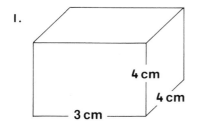

2.

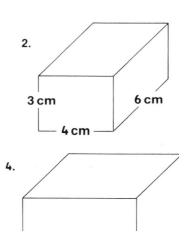

3.

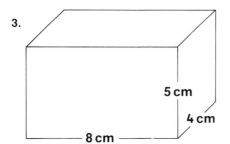

4.

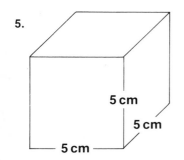

5.

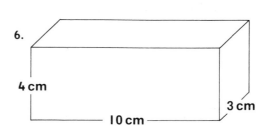

6.

87

Fractions

Find:

1. $\frac{3}{4}$ of 488 g
2. $\frac{3}{8}$ of 2·40 m
3. $\frac{5}{6}$ of £2·40
4. $\frac{1}{6}$ of 372

5. $\frac{2}{3}$ of 189 kg
6. $\frac{3}{5}$ of £1·35
7. $\frac{7}{10}$ of 940 l
8. $\frac{2}{5}$ of 725 ml

9. $\frac{3}{7}$ of 2506
10. $\frac{7}{8}$ of 712 cm
11. $\frac{1}{2}$ of £38·52
12. $\frac{2}{9}$ of 405

13. $\frac{9}{10}$ of 1210 g
14. $\frac{5}{6}$ of 948 kg
15. $\frac{5}{7}$ of £66·78
16. $\frac{5}{8}$ of 8·96 m

17. At the football match there were 7032 people.
One quarter of the people were children.
How many adults were at the match?

18. The admission charge for an adult was £3.50.
Children were charged $\frac{3}{5}$ of that amount.
What was the admission charge for a child?

19. A man on a stall outside the ground sold £139 worth of goods.
Three quarters of the money received was for flags.
How much did the man receive for the flags?

20. On a refreshment stand, a man took £132.
One quarter of the money received was for drinks, $\frac{1}{3}$ for ice-creams,
and the remainder for food snacks.
How much money was spent on each group of items?

> When adding mixed numbers, add the whole ones first.

$2\frac{1}{2} + 1\frac{2}{3}$

$= 3\frac{1}{2} + \frac{2}{3}$

$= 3\frac{3}{6} + \frac{4}{6}$

$= 3\frac{7}{6}$

$= 4\frac{1}{6}$

1. $1\frac{3}{4} + 2\frac{1}{3}$

2. $3\frac{1}{2} + 1\frac{7}{10}$

3. $4\frac{2}{5} + \frac{2}{3}$

4. $5\frac{2}{3} + 2\frac{1}{2}$

5. $1\frac{5}{8} + 3\frac{1}{3}$

6. $2\frac{1}{4} + 1\frac{4}{5}$

7. $3\frac{7}{10} + 1\frac{3}{4}$

8. $2\frac{5}{6} + 3\frac{3}{4}$

9. $5\frac{2}{3} + 1\frac{3}{4}$

10. $1\frac{2}{3} + 3\frac{5}{8}$

11. $4\frac{4}{9} + 3\frac{5}{6}$

12. $1\frac{2}{3} + 5\frac{7}{8}$

13. $2\frac{1}{8} + 4\frac{1}{2}$

14. $1\frac{1}{2} + 2\frac{5}{8}$

15. $3\frac{6}{7} + 2\frac{1}{2}$

16. $2\frac{1}{2} + 3\frac{5}{8}$

17. $1\frac{2}{3} + 2\frac{3}{4}$

18. $3\frac{7}{8} + 1\frac{1}{3}$

19. $2\frac{7}{10} + 1\frac{1}{2}$

20. $3\frac{4}{5} + 1\frac{2}{3}$

21. $1\frac{7}{8} + 2\frac{3}{4}$

22. $3\frac{3}{10} + 1\frac{4}{5}$

23. $4\frac{1}{3} + 1\frac{5}{12}$

24. $4\frac{2}{3} + 1\frac{1}{4} + 2\frac{5}{12}$

25. $1\frac{3}{4} + 2\frac{3}{8} + \frac{1}{3}$

26. $2\frac{5}{6} + 3\frac{1}{4} + 1\frac{5}{12}$

27. $3\frac{3}{10} + 1\frac{1}{2} + \frac{4}{5}$

28. $2\frac{1}{2} + 1\frac{1}{3} + 1\frac{5}{12}$

29. $2\frac{1}{10} + 3\frac{2}{3} + 4\frac{4}{5}$

Decimals

Make these numbers 10 times bigger.

1. 6
2. 40
3. 8
4. 71
5. 124
6. 235
7. 17
8. 407
9. 600
10. 101

Make these numbers 10 times smaller.

11. 30
12. 70
13. 610
14. 1480
15. 90
16. 100
17. 2010
18. 1560
19. 700
20. 1000

Make these numbers 100 times bigger.

21. 2
22. 14
23. 89
24. 94
25. 140
26. 600
27. 73
28. 100
29. 842
30. 69

Make these numbers 100 times smaller.

31. 100
32. 200
33. 3700
34. 9000
35. 700
36. 1600
37. 1400
38. 8300
39. 4200
40. 300
41. 1900
42. 9900
43. 7700
44. 6800
45. 1200

1000 made 10 times smaller is 100
100 made 10 times smaller is 10
10 made 10 times smaller is 1
1 made 10 times smaller is $\frac{1}{10}$

Th	H	T	U	$\frac{1}{10}$
1	0	0	0 ·	0
	1	0	0 ·	0
		1	0 ·	0
			1 ·	0
			0 ·	1

The **decimal point** separates the whole number from the fraction.

$\frac{1}{10}$ is written 0·1

$1\frac{3}{10}$ is written 1·3

Write these fractions as decimals.

1. $1\frac{7}{10}$
2. $2\frac{4}{10}$
3. $4\frac{5}{10}$
4. $\frac{3}{10}$
5. $3\frac{9}{10}$

6. $29\frac{6}{10}$
7. $30\frac{3}{10}$
8. $\frac{7}{10}$
9. $107\frac{1}{10}$
10. $49\frac{8}{10}$

Write these fractions as tenths. Then change to decimals.

11. $2\frac{1}{2}$
12. $5\frac{2}{5}$
13. $16\frac{4}{5}$
14. $98\frac{3}{5}$
15. $206\frac{1}{2}$

Write these decimals as fractions.

16. 1·4
17. 3·2
18. 4·1
19. 2·9
20. 5·8

21. 1·7
22. 0·4
23. 7·3
24. 0·5
25. 67·3

26. 49·1
27. 17·9
28. 102·5
29. 417·7
30. 200·6

31. 73·2
32. 46·9
33. 88·8
34. 94·5
35. 32·1

Make these numbers 10 times bigger.

36. 0·1
37. 1·4
38. 2·5
39. 6·8
40. 9·2

41. 14·7
42. 62·8
43. 29·1
44. 17·8
45. 49·6

46. 87·4
47. 107·6
48. 216·3
49. 300·1
50. 450·5

51. 603·1
52. 289·5
53. 703·4
54. 810·9
55. 515·1

Make these numbers 10 times smaller.

56. 29
57. 41
58. 37
59. 62
60. 94

61. 104
62. 87
63. 242
64. 617
65. 409

66. 810
67. 1241
68. 6298
69. 7241
70. 4905

71. 11
72. 24
73. 32
74. 2938
75. 1809

Measurement

Balance (or scales), marbles, measuring jug, sand

Find the weight of 750 ml of water.
Remember to first weigh the container empty.
Calculate the weight of $1\frac{1}{2}$ l of water.

Weigh a litre of sand.
Calculate the weight of a 10 l bucket
full of sand.

Weigh 10 marbles.
Calculate the weight of 1 marble.
Calculate the weight of 100 marbles.

How many marbles weigh 50 g?
Calculate how many marbles there are in 500 g.
Calculate how many marbles there are in 1 kg.

1. John buys a set of 8 books. Each book is 39 mm thick.
   What is the total thickness of the set of books?

2. Anita cycles to school and back home each day.
   She stays at school for lunch.
   She cycles 21 km each week.
   How far from school is her home?

3. Barry bought a litre bottle of lemonade.
   He drank 277 ml from it.
   He then shared the remainder equally among three friends.
   How much did they each receive?

4. Jane's father weighs 78 kg. She weighs $\frac{1}{3}$ of his weight.
   How much does she weigh?

5. Gwen put 25 l of petrol in her car. Petrol costs £2·14 for 5 l.
   How much did she have to pay?

6. The school gate is 2 m wide. A delivery van is 1·47 m wide.
   How many centimetres are there to spare?

7. Which is the better buy and how much would be saved?

Shape

Paper circle, string, tin lid

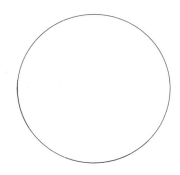

Find the centre of the paper circle by folding.
Mark the centre with a coloured pencil.
How do you know the mark is the centre?
Measure the lines you have made.

≫ Each line measures ☐ cm.

The distance from the edge of the circle to the centre is called its **radius**.

When there is more than one radius, we say **radii**.

The perimeter of a circle is called its **circumference**.

Stick your paper circle in your book.
Label the circumference, radius and diameter.

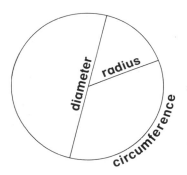

Find a tin lid.
Use string to measure its circumference.

Before using the compasses,
make sure that the pencil point
and compass point are level.

Open the compasses to 4 cm.
Draw a circle using the compasses.

≫ This circle has a radius of ☐ cm.

Draw circles that have radii
of 5 cm, 7 cm and 3 cm.

Now use the compasses to draw circle patterns.

Number

Mr. Jones hires out cars.
He has five cars for people to choose from.
This table shows how many miles each car will travel on 5 litres of petrol.

Car No. 1	Car No. 2	Car No. 3	Car No. 4	Car No. 5
28 miles	29 miles	34 miles	38 miles	44 miles

Each car has 30 litres of petrol in it.

1. Make a table to show how far each car would travel on the petrol already in it.

2. Mr. Smith hired Car No. 2.
   His journey was 116 miles each way.
   How much more petrol would he need?

3. Mr. James was travelling 300 miles altogether.
   He could only afford 10 litres of petrol.
   Which cars could he choose?

4. Mr. Martin chose Car No. 1.
   Mr. Richards chose Car No. 4.
   They put another 30 litres in each car.
   How much further could Mr. Richards travel than Mr. Martin?

5. Make another table to show how far each car would travel on 50 litres of petrol.
   Draw a stick graph from the table.

96

John and Robert each have a bank book.
The books show how much each of them has in the bank.
When they take money out of the bank, it is a **withdrawal**.
When they put money in the bank, it is a **deposit**.
The amount they have in the bank is the **balance**.

These pictures show a page in each of their bank books.

John's bank book

Date	Deposit £	Withdrawal £	Balance £
May 1st			50 00
4th	6 40		
6th		9 50	
14th	3 75		
15th	12 45		
22nd		7 20	
24th		6 38	
29th	4 45		
31st		6 95	

Robert's bank book

Date	Deposit £	Withdrawal £	Balance £
May 1st			50 00
6th		7 32	
9th	12 05		
12th		6 55	
16th	1 75		
22nd	4 45		
29th		4 80	
30th		1 95	
31st		1 58	

Each had £50 in the bank at the beginning of the month.
Copy the two bank book pages into your book.
Work out the balance after each entry in the bank book.

1. Who had the larger balance at the end of the month?

2. How much more did he have than his friend?

Area

Calculate the area of these rectangles.

1. 7 cm by 5 cm
2. 12 cm × 6 cm
3. 14 cm × 10 cm
4. 26 cm by 9 cm
5. 19 cm × 8 cm
6. 18 cm × 7 cm

7.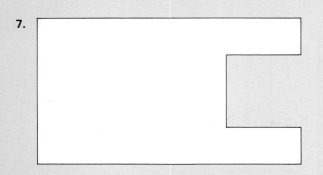

8.

To measure a large area we use a square, I metre by I metre.
A square, I m by I m, has an area of I **square metre**.
We write it as I **m²**.

9. Use your metre stick to draw I m² on the classroom floor.
   Estimate the area of the classroom in m².
   Measure the length of the classroom in metres (to the nearest metre).
   Measure the width of the classroom in metres (to the nearest metre).
   Calculate the approximate area of the classroom in m².

10. In the same way, find the area of the hall, or the library, or the playground, or any other room in the school.

11. How many cm² make I m²?

Calculate the area of:

1. a rectangular table 2 m by 1 m.
2. a sheet of paper 10 cm by 24 cm.
3. a carpet 6 m by 5 m.
4. a piece of card 9 cm by 14 cm.

Find the length of:

5. a rectangle of area 80 cm² and width 5 cm.
6. a carpet of area 15 m² and width 5 m.
7. a garden of area 189 m² and width 9 m.

Calculate the area of each of these plots of land.
The scale for each drawing is shown.

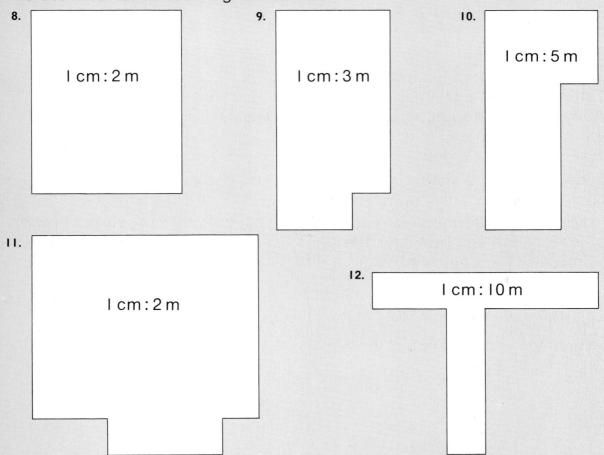

8.

1 cm : 2 m

9.

1 cm : 3 m

10.

1 cm : 5 m

11.

1 cm : 2 m

12.

1 cm : 10 m

Mr. Giles is a farmer.
These are plans of two of his fields.
They are drawn to scale.
Every 1 cm represents 10 m (1 cm : 10 m).

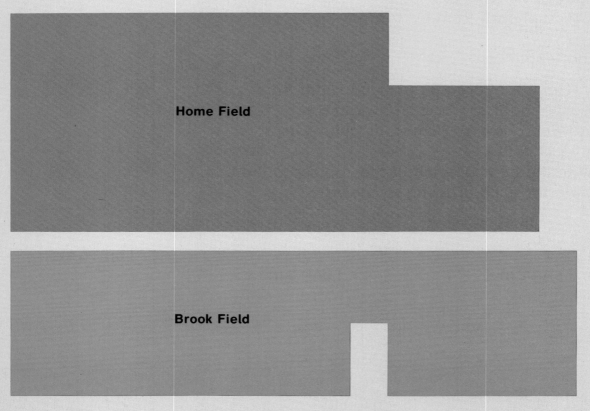

Home Field

Brook Field

1. Calculate the perimeter of each field.

2. If fencing costs £2 for each 10 m, how much will it cost Mr. Giles to fence both fields?

Mrs. Giles looks after the garden.
This is a plan of it.
The scale is 1 cm : 2 m.

1. What is the area of
   Mrs. Giles' garden?

2. A lawn takes up $\frac{1}{2}$ of
   Mrs. Giles' garden.
   What is the area of the lawn?

3. Vegetables take up $\frac{1}{4}$ of
   the garden.
   What area is taken up by vegetables?

4. Flowers take up $\frac{1}{6}$ of the garden.
   What area is taken up by flowers?

5. The rest of the garden is taken up by paths.
   What area of the garden do the paths cover?

Volume

Number of cubes in a layer   20
Number of layers   6
Volume   120 cm³

Area of base   20 cm²
Height   6 cm
Volume   120 cm³

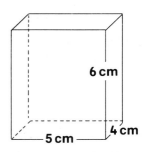

The volume of a cuboid can be found by multiplying the area of its base by its height.

Calculate the volumes of these boxes.
Write your answers like this:

$$\text{Area of base} = \boxed{} \text{ cm}^2$$
$$\text{Height} = \boxed{} \text{ cm}$$
$$\text{Volume} = \boxed{} \text{ cm}^3$$

1.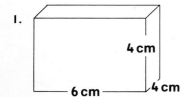

2.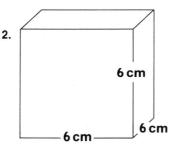

3.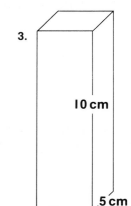

4.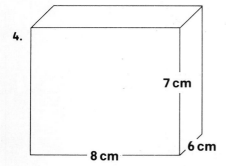

5.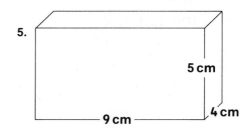

1. The volume is 60 cm³.
   What is the area of its base?
   What is the width?

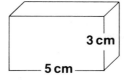

2. The volume is 120 cm³.
   What is the area of its base?
   What is the length?

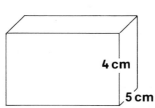

3. The volume is 180 cm³.
   What is the area of its base?
   What is the length?

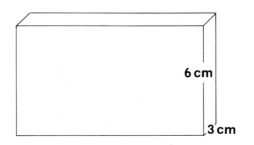

4. The volume is 360 cm³.
   What is the width?

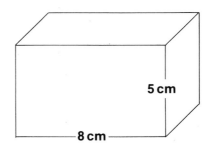

5. The volume is 210 cm³.
   What is the length?

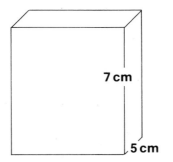

Graphs

Mr. North has a hot air balloon. He travels long distances in it.
It travels at a steady 10 km an hour. (1 km = 1000 m)

He set off one day at noon for an 8 hour flight.
This table shows how far he travelled each hour.

Time	Noon	1 pm	2 pm	3 pm	4 pm	5 pm	6 pm	7 pm	8 pm
Distance travelled in km	0	10	20	30	40	50	60	70	80

Copy this graph into your book.

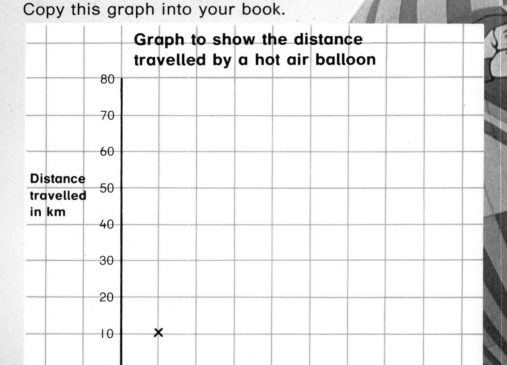

Graph to show the distance travelled by a hot air balloon

The point that is plotted shows how far
the balloon had travelled by 1 pm.
Plot the points for each hour up to 8 pm.
Join the points with a straight line.
You have drawn a **line graph**.

The school photographer visited David's school.
He took a photograph of each class.
He sold them for £1.50 each.

This graph helped the teachers to find quickly how much each class had to pay for photographs.

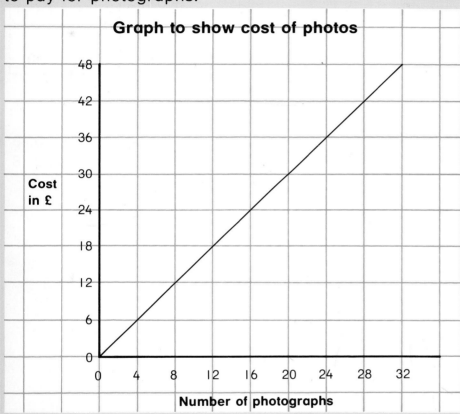

Graph to show cost of photos

Answer these questions from the graph.

1. Mrs. Brown's class bought 24 photos.
   How much did she collect from the class?

2. Mrs. Hanbury's class had 32 photos. How much did she collect?

3. Mr. Bond's class only bought 16 photos. How much did his class pay?

4. Mr. Straw's class had 20 photos. How much did he collect?

5. Mrs. Smith's class bought 30 photos. How much did her class pay?

Decimals

Add these:

```
    1·5         1.    0·2        2.    3·4        3.    2·5        4.    6·3
  + 2·6            + 1·7            + 1·5            + 1·8            + 0·7
  ─────            ─────            ─────            ─────            ─────
    4·1
  ─────            ─────            ─────            ─────            ─────
```

```
 5.   0·6        6.   29·4       7.    3·5        8.   62·3        9.   59·7
    + 0·7           + 18·7          + 42·9           + 27·7           + 27·6
    ─────           ──────          ──────           ──────           ──────


    ─────           ──────          ──────           ──────           ──────
```

```
10.  102·7       11.   594·7      12.   399·8      13.   605·3
   + 311·4          + 327·8          + 410·6          + 160·8
   ──────           ──────           ──────           ──────


   ──────           ──────           ──────           ──────
```

Subtract these:

```
    2·7        14.   4·3        15.   6·7        16.   2·3        17.   3·5
  - 1·8            - 1·2            - 2·5            - 1·7            - 1·9
  ─────            ─────            ─────            ─────            ─────
    0·9
  ─────            ─────            ─────            ─────            ─────
```

```
18.   3·0        19.   24·6       20.   14·4       21.   67·1       22.   82·7
    - 1·2            - 13·9           -  0·7           - 29·2           - 59·8
    ─────           ──────           ──────           ──────           ──────


    ─────           ──────           ──────           ──────           ──────
```

```
23.   301·6      24.   427·3      25.   400·8      26.   490·5
    - 200·9          - 189·5          - 215·9          - 172·6
    ──────           ──────           ──────           ──────


    ──────           ──────           ──────           ──────
```

Multiply these:

	27·4	1.	48·7	2.	69·6	3.	14·7	4.	58·1
×	5	×	3	×	9	×	6	×	3
	137·0								

5. 90·7
× 8

6. 122·4
× 5

7. 404·7
× 4

8. 692·2
× 6

9. 472·9
× 7

10. 629·4
× 9

11. 1242·7
× 4

12. 2039·8
× 3

13. 1105·8
× 8

14. 1162·4
× 6

15. 2602·2
× 3

16. 408·9
× 9

Divide these:

    12·3
4) 49·2

17. 6) 138·6

18. 3) 135·3

19. 8) 454·4

20. 5) 206·0

21. 7) 639·1

22. 4) 154·0

23. 9) 525·6

24. 6) 453·0

25. 8) 652·8

26. 5) 767·5

27. 7) 3586·8

28. 9) 303·3

29. 4) 623·2

30. 9) 1818·9

31. 5) 4505·5

Measurement

Measure these lines to the nearest cm.
Use string to help you.

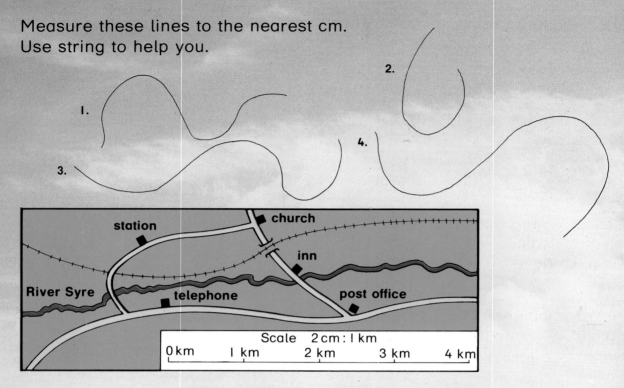

5. How far is it from the church to the inn?

6. How far is it from the station to the post office?

7. How far is it from the inn to the telephone?

8. How far is it from the post office to where the railway passes over the road?

9. How much further is it from the church to the telephone via the post office than via the station?

This chart shows the distances, in miles, between the towns shown. The coloured square shows that Leeds and Liverpool are 75 miles apart.

Newcastle-upon-Tyne	Inverness	Kendal	Leeds	Leicester	Lincoln	Liverpool	Manchester
268							
84	294						
92	360	71					
187	462	160	95				
159	427	136	68	51			
155	382	72	75	100	118		
132	373	72	40	92	84	35	

1. How far is it from Manchester to Inverness?

2. How far is it from Kendal to Newcastle-upon-Tyne?

3. I travel from Leeds to Leicester, then on to Lincoln.
   How far have I gone?

Here is a map showing the distances, in kilometres, between five towns.

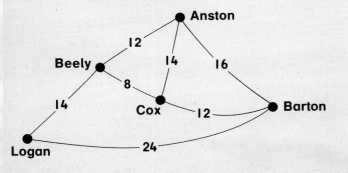

4. Copy and complete this chart showing the shortest distances between the towns.

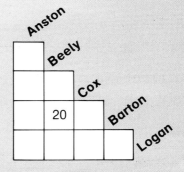

Anston	Beely	Cox	Barton	Logan
		20		

Number

1. Find the total of these numbers.

2. Find the difference between the largest and smallest numbers.

3. Find the average of these numbers.

4. Write which of them divide exactly by 4.

5. Find what needs to be added to the total to make 10000.

6. Find $\frac{3}{4}$ of the largest number.

7. Find $\frac{2}{3}$ of the smallest number.

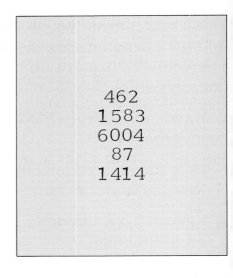

```
  462
 1583
 6004
   87
 1414
```

8. Find the total of these amounts.

9. Which amount is 48p less than £10?

10. Which amount is double another amount?

11. Which two amounts, when added, come to less than £5?

12. Subtract the next to the smallest amount from the largest amount.

13. Find the average of the five amounts.

```
£8.70
£6.08
£9.52
£4.35
£0.60
```

This dial shows the miles travelled by a car.

14. Its last journey was 189 miles.
What did the dial show before that journey?

15. The average mileage travelled each week is 100 miles.
How many weeks old is the car?

16. Its next journey will be 104 miles.
What will the dial show then?

The sign $>$ means is **greater than**.
The sign $<$ means is **less than**.

$$7 + 4 > 9$$
$$19 - 4 < 6 \times 4$$

Put the correct sign $> < =$ in these:

1. $17 + 34 \;\square\; 7 \times 7$

2. $3 \times 56 \;\square\; 144 + 27$

3. $600 - 145 \;\square\; 700 - 245$

4. $500 \div 4 \;\square\; 1000 \div 8$

5. $700 \div 2 \;\square\; \frac{1}{2}$ of 698

6. $\frac{1}{8}$ of $96 \;\square\; 96 \div 8$

7. $\frac{1}{3}$ of $60 \;\square\; 9 \times 3$

8. $40 \times 6 \;\square\; 252 \div 6$

Use the examples to help you do these:

$$
\begin{array}{r}
345 \\
+\,197 \\
\hline
542 \\
\end{array}
$$

9. $542 - 197$

10. $197 + 345$

11. $542 - 345$

$$
\begin{array}{r}
502 \\
-\,247 \\
\hline
255 \\
\end{array}
$$

12. $247 + 255$

13. $502 - 255$

14. $255 + 247$

15. Find a number which is 9 times greater than 896.

16. Which number is $\frac{2}{3}$ of 1683?

17. Find a number which is $\frac{3}{4}$ of 6464.

18. Add together $\frac{1}{3}$ of £17·10 and $\frac{3}{8}$ of £19·60.

19. Which sum of money is worth 6 times £4·85?

20. How many times will 7 divide into 3843?

21. Find the average of 2121, 3608, 400, 3931.

22. What is the average of £7·35, £8·42, £0·16, £3·84, £2·08?

23. The product of two numbers is 196.
    One of the numbers is 7. Find the other number.

Graphs

These grapes cost 75p a bunch.
Complete this table showing the cost of bunches of grapes.

No. of bunches	1	2	3	4	5
Cost in £	0·75				

Copy these axes and draw a line graph, showing the cost of grapes.

This table shows the cost of peaches.

No. of peaches	2	4	6	8	10	12	14	16	18
Cost in £	0·50	1·00	1·50	2·00	2·50	3·00	3·50	4·00	4·50

Draw a line graph of the information shown.
From the graph, find the cost of:

1. 5 peaches.   2. 9 peaches.   3. 13 peaches.   4. 17 peaches.

Mr. Leggit is a long-distance walker.
He walks 5 miles in an hour.
He set off one Saturday to walk from Derby to Sheffield.
The distance he had to walk was 40 miles.
This is the route he took. The numbers show the miles between towns.

| ⊢——8——⊢——2——⊢——8——⊢————7——⊢——2——⊢————13————⊣ |
| Derby   Belper Ambergate   Matlock   Chatsworth Baslow   Sheffield |

1. Complete this table to show how far he travelled each hour.

No. of hours	1	2	3	4	5	6	7	8
Distance in miles	5	10						

2. Draw a line graph of the distance travelled each hour.

Answer these questions from the graph.

3. How far had he walked in
   a) $3\frac{1}{2}$ hrs?   b) $6\frac{1}{2}$ hrs?

4. How long did it take him to walk
   a) $12\frac{1}{2}$ miles?   b) $37\frac{1}{2}$ miles?

Answer these questions from the plan
of the route.

5. How long did it take him to walk
   a) from Derby to Ambergate?
   b) from Ambergate to Chatsworth?
   c) from Chatsworth to Sheffield?

6. If he left Derby at 10 o'clock, at what time
   did he reach
   a) Belper?   b) Chatsworth?   c) Baslow?

Angles

Cm squared paper

Measure these angles.

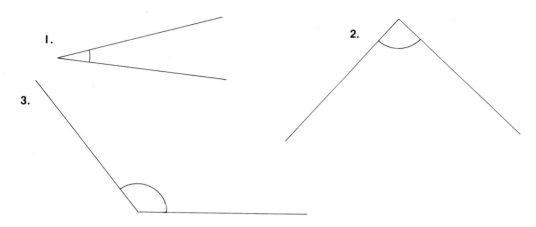

1.

2.

3.

Draw these angles.

4. 79°   5. 108°   6. 171°   7. 16°   8. 42°

Write beside each angle whether it is acute or obtuse.

On squared paper draw the axes and label
them as shown in the diagram.

Join up these co-ordinates.
9. (8.1) (2.2) (5.9)
Measure the angle and give its name.

Now do the same for these:

10. (9.2) (4.1) (1.6)
11. (1.4) (6.8) (5.1)
12. (1.8) (8.5) (6.1)
13. (4.1) (2.8) (7.2)

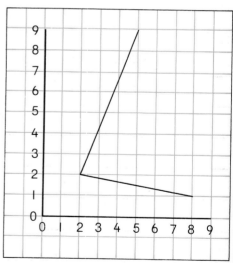

14. On squared paper label axes 0 to 7.
    Draw the triangle whose co-ordinates are: (1.1) (3.6) (6.2)
    Measure each angle.

Write the name of each triangle.

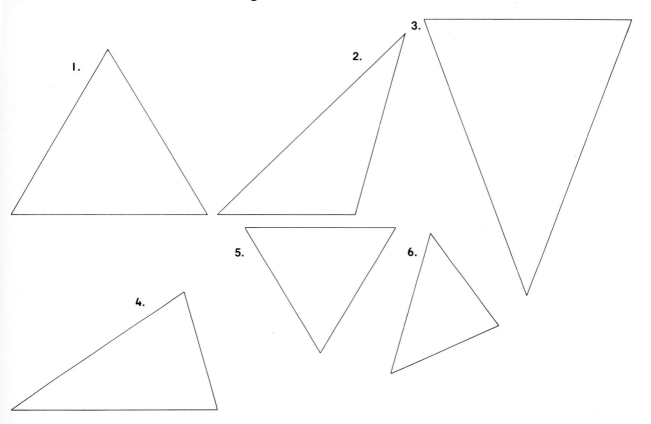

7. Draw this table.
   Now measure the angles of each triangle and total them.

Triangle No.	Degrees in each angle	Total
I	60° + 60° + 60°	180°

≫ The angles of a triangle add up to ☐.

115

Investigations

25 pin geo-board, spotty paper

Halve your geo-board by stretching an elastic band
from one side to the other.
The same number of pins must be each side of the band.

How many different ways can you find of halving the board?
Record your results on spotty paper.

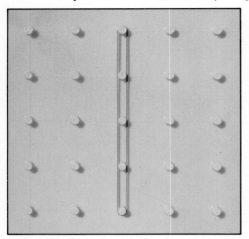 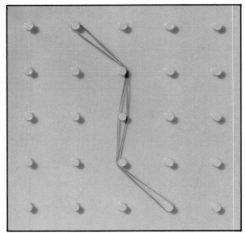

Quarter your geo-board by stretching two elastic bands
across the board.

How many different ways can you find of quartering the board?
Record your results on spotty paper.

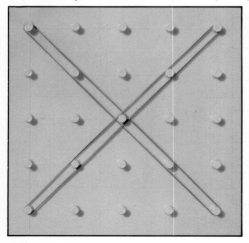 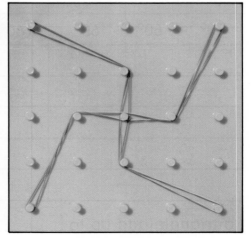

Matchsticks, counters, squared paper

Puzzle it out.

Take away 5 matchsticks to leave 3 squares of the same size.

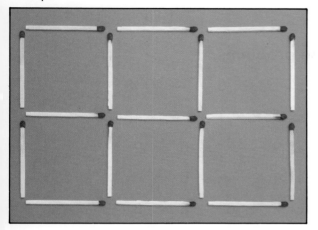

Copy this star without taking your pencil off the paper and without going over the same line twice.

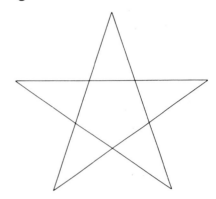

Copy this into your book.
Draw 3 straight lines which will separate the 7 mice from each other.

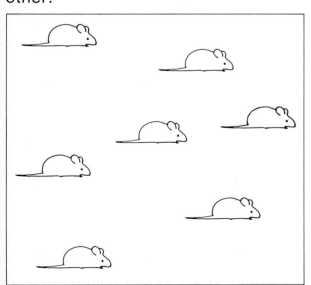

Rearrange the counters so that no more than 2 counters are in a straight line.

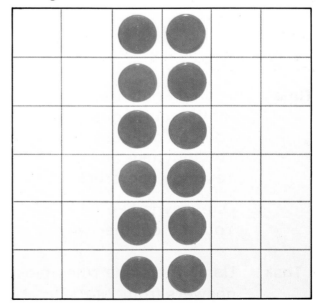

Number problems

$(4 \times 3) - 2 = 10$

When you have part of a number problem inside brackets you must work that part out first.

$(4 \times 3) - 2 = 10$
$12 - 2 = 10$

$(16 - 4) - (4 + 3) = 5$
$12 - 7 = 5$

Find where to put the brackets in these problems.

1. $8 + 6 \times 2 = 28$
2. $15 - 3 + 4 = 8$
3. $20 + 12 \div 3 = 24$
4. $13 - 1 \div 4 = 3$
5. $5 + 3 \times 4 = 32$
6. $9 - 2 \times 0 = 9$
7. $6 \times 5 - 3 = 27$
8. $4 \div 4 \times 0 = 0$
9. $19 - 3 \times 5 = 4$
10. $7 + 8 \div 8 = 8$
11. $10 + 2 \times 6 - 4 = 18$
12. $36 - 16 \div 4 + 8 = 40$
13. $12 + 4 \div 24 \div 3 = 2$
14. $9 \times 8 + 4 \times 7 = 100$
15. $7 + 1 \div 3 + 5 = 1$
16. $2 \times 6 - 4 + 4 = 4$
17. $18 + 3 - 7 \div 7 = 2$
18. $6 \times 3 \div 9 \times 0 = 0$

Task Make up a number problem to give an answer of 1.

Rules You can only use the digits 1, 2, 3 and 4.
All the four digits must be used.
You can only use each digit once.
You may use any of the signs $+ - \times \div$.
You may use brackets.

One way is like this: $(3 + 2) - (4 \times 1)$
You find another way.

Task Using the same rules make up number problems to give answers from 2 to 12.

Divide these numbers by 10.

1. 460   2. 610   3. 4800   4. 2620   5. 7460   6. 3270

There is no remainder.
We say the numbers are **exactly divisible** by 10.
Write the rule which tells you when a number is exactly divisible by 10.

Which of these numbers are exactly divisible by 5?

7. 495   8. 366   9. 2740   10. 3775   11. 4163   12. 5360

Write the rule which tells you when a number is exactly divisible by 5.

Which of these numbers are exactly divisible by 4?

13. 736   14. 612   15. 331   16. 1540   17. 7322   18. 3016

Look carefully at the last two digits of the numbers.
Write the rule which tells you when a number is exactly divisible by 4.

Leap year dates are divisible by 4.
Use this rule to find out which of these events happened in a leap year.

1431
Joan of Arc
burnt at the stake

1564
William Shakespeare
born

1666
Great Fire of London

1776
American Declaration of
Independence from Britain

1840
Penny postage introduced

1953
Coronation of
Queen Elizabeth II

4 red counters, 4 yellow counters

Put 4 red counters on the top row.
Put 4 yellow counters on the bottom row.

Task   To change the positions of the red and yellow counters.

Rules   Counters can move one place at a time.
They can only move into empty spaces.
They cannot jump each other.

Strips of paper

Make a hoop with a paper strip.

If you cut along the centre of the strip what will happen?
See if you were correct.

Make another hoop but put a twist in the paper first.
What will happen if you cut along the centre of the strip?
See if you were correct.

Put two twists in a hoop and repeat what you have been doing.

Number – more practice

1. 648 + 2719   2. 5784 + 3297   3. 1728 + 29

4. 636 + 1978   5. 4037 + 94   6. 1319 + 7218

7. 4062 + 361 + 2984   8. 5131 + 19 + 2983

9. 27 + 2969 + 1008   10. 731 + 1946 + 5446

11. Find the total of 7293 and 1987.

12. Increase 2618 by 3964.

13. To 1628 add 3986.

14. 4206 − 1783   15. 3321 − 1793   16. 4907 − 259

17. 6003 − 1878   18. 4621 − 89   19. 3408 − 1794

20. 5000 − 3934   21. 9036 − 4862   22. 6202 − 2844

23. Find the difference between 387 and 1042.

24. Subtract 1936 from 4600.

25. How much less than 2861 is 1974?

26. 1606 × 6   27. 948 × 8   28. 1374 × 5   29. 2847 × 4

30. 1926 × 4   31. 1038 × 7   32. 648 × 10   33. 3949 × 2

34. Multiply 4628 by 2.

35. Find the product of 7 and 268.

36. Which number is 8 times greater than 747?

37. 4032 ÷ 6   38. 8742 ÷ 9   39. 3717 ÷ 10   40. 4964 ÷ 4

41. 7077 ÷ 8   42. 6135 ÷ 5   43. 6545 ÷ 7   44. 4131 ÷ 3

45. Divide 6498 by 9.

46. How many 4s are there in 3844?

Money – more practice

1. £4·72 + £3·46
2. £8·08 + £5·94
3. £6·29 + £0·95
4. £9·62 + £5·59
5. £0·89 + £3·65
6. £4·88 + £3·72
7. £1·64 + 74p + £0·97
8. £2·68 + £5·42 + £1·95
9. 38p + £2·74 + £5·68
10. £6·66 + £2·95 + £4·73

11. Find the total of £2·75, £1·38 and 95p.

12. To £7·58 add £9·79.

13. Add together £3·84, £0·72 and £5·05.

14. £3·84 − £1·75
15. £2·62 − £0·59
16. £3·05 − £0·87
17. £6·00 − £2·72
18. £14·80 − £2·97
19. £5·48 − 75p
20. £13·65 − £9·38
21. £6·50 − 95p
22. £10·50 − £3·85

23. Find the difference between £10 and £6.35.

24. How much less than £7·80 is £4·95?

25. How much is needed to make £3·45 into £7·50?

26. £1·48 × 2
27. £3·19 × 7
28. £0·56 × 5
29. £5·45 × 6
30. £8·95 × 9
31. £9·39 × 3
32. £1·83 × 4
33. 96p × 10

34. Multiply £6·35 by 7.

35. What amount is 6 times greater than £4·25?

36. Find the value of 5 amounts of £3·75.

37. £17·22 ÷ 2
38. £36·95 ÷ 5
39. £18·40 ÷ 10
40. £4·76 ÷ 7
41. £10·53 ÷ 9
42. £17·36 ÷ 4
43. £16·24 ÷ 8
44. £14·31 ÷ 3

45. Divide £14·72 by 8.

46. Find $\frac{1}{10}$ of £19·70.

Fractions – more practice

1. $\frac{4}{5} + \frac{1}{10}$

2. $\frac{1}{3} + \frac{3}{10}$

3. $\frac{3}{4} + \frac{2}{5}$

4. $\frac{7}{8} + \frac{1}{3} + \frac{1}{2}$

5. $\frac{3}{5} + \frac{1}{2} + \frac{9}{10}$

6. $\frac{5}{8} + \frac{2}{3} + \frac{3}{4}$

7. $1\frac{3}{8} + \frac{1}{2}$

8. $2\frac{1}{3} + 1\frac{1}{4}$

9. $1\frac{1}{6} + 2\frac{7}{12}$

10. $2\frac{2}{5} + 1\frac{2}{3}$

11. $\frac{7}{10} + 2\frac{1}{2}$

12. $3\frac{2}{5} + 1\frac{3}{4}$

13. $4\frac{11}{12} + \frac{2}{3}$

14. $3\frac{7}{8} + 1\frac{3}{5}$

15. $1\frac{5}{8} + 2\frac{3}{4}$

16. $1\frac{9}{10} + 2\frac{5}{6}$

17. $2\frac{3}{4} + \frac{7}{10}$

18. $1\frac{5}{12} + 2\frac{2}{3}$

19. $\frac{2}{3} - \frac{1}{4}$

20. $\frac{7}{10} - \frac{2}{5}$

21. $\frac{7}{12} - \frac{1}{3}$

22. $\frac{5}{8} - \frac{1}{3}$

23. $\frac{3}{4} - \frac{2}{5}$

24. $\frac{9}{10} - \frac{2}{3}$

25. $\frac{4}{5} - \frac{1}{4}$

26. $\frac{5}{6} - \frac{5}{12}$

27. $\frac{7}{8} - \frac{1}{6}$

28. $\frac{1}{2} - \frac{2}{5}$

29. $\frac{3}{4} - \frac{7}{12}$

30. $\frac{5}{6} - \frac{3}{8}$

31. Find $\frac{3}{4}$ of £6.

32. How much is $\frac{2}{5}$ of £7·35?

33. Which number is $\frac{3}{8}$ of 1768?

34. What weight is $\frac{1}{4}$ of 2 kg?

35. What is $\frac{7}{8}$ of 10 l?

36. How much greater is $\frac{3}{4}$ of 1 l than $\frac{1}{4}$ of 2 l?

37. Take $\frac{1}{4}$ of 3 kg from $\frac{2}{3}$ of 6 kg.

38. Add $\frac{1}{2}$ of 7 m to 3·65 m.

124

Measurement – more practice

1. $2.64 \text{ m} + 1.38 \text{ m}$
2. $0.72 \text{ m} + 1.68 \text{ m}$
3. $75 \text{ cm} + 2.38 \text{ m}$
4. $1.62 \text{ m} + 3.95 \text{ m} + 50 \text{ cm}$
5. $6.05 \text{ m} + 2.85 \text{ m} + 1.75 \text{ m}$
6. $3.62 \text{ m} - 1.85 \text{ m}$
7. $4 \text{ m} - 2.25 \text{ m}$
8. $5.38 \text{ m} - 80 \text{ cm}$
9. $8.63 \text{ m} - 3.96 \text{ m}$
10. $5.70 \text{ m} - 96 \text{ cm}$
11. $2.27 \text{ m} - 1.93 \text{ m}$
12. $1.48 \text{ m} \times 2$
13. $65 \text{ cm} \times 7$
14. $4.38 \text{ m} \times 8$
15. $2.59 \text{ m} \times 9$
16. $3.38 \text{ m} \times 6$
17. $4.95 \text{ m} \times 5$
18. $3.51 \text{ m} \div 3$
19. $5.70 \text{ m} \div 10$
20. $6.75 \text{ m} \div 9$
21. $4.56 \text{ m} \div 8$
22. $3.66 \text{ m} \div 6$
23. $8.19 \text{ m} \div 7$

24. $1\frac{1}{4} \text{ kg} + 750 \text{ g}$
25. $1\frac{1}{2} \text{ kg} + 500 \text{ g}$
26. $650 \text{ g} + 2\frac{1}{2} \text{ kg}$
27. $3 \text{ kg} - 800 \text{ g}$
28. $2 \text{ kg} - 400 \text{ g}$
29. $2\frac{1}{2} \text{ kg} - 350 \text{ g}$
30. $500 \text{ ml} + 1\frac{1}{4} \text{ l}$
31. $2\frac{1}{2} \text{ l} + 750 \text{ ml}$
32. $1\frac{3}{4} \text{ l} + 500 \text{ ml}$
33. $2 \text{ l} - 500 \text{ ml}$
34. $1\frac{1}{2} \text{ l} - 350 \text{ ml}$
35. $1 \text{ l} - 625 \text{ ml}$

Write the answers to these in kg.

36. $350 \text{ g} \times 6$
37. $420 \text{ g} \times 7$
38. $325 \text{ g} \times 9$
39. $525 \text{ g} \times 8$
40. $725 \text{ g} \times 5$
41. $850 \text{ g} \times 4$
42. $750 \text{ g} \times 3$
43. $395 \text{ g} \times 6$

Write the answers to these in l.

44. $730 \text{ ml} \times 8$
45. $630 \text{ ml} \times 7$
46. $835 \text{ ml} \times 6$
47. $500 \text{ ml} \times 5$
48. $965 \text{ ml} \times 10$
49. $635 \text{ ml} \times 9$
50. $875 \text{ ml} \times 2$
51. $455 \text{ ml} \times 6$
52. $395 \text{ ml} \times 8$

53. How many ml in $\frac{2}{5}$ of 2 l?

54. How many ml in $\frac{1}{8}$ of 1 l?

55. How many cm in $\frac{3}{10}$ of 2 m?

56. How many cm in $\frac{4}{5}$ of 1 m?

Assessment

1. $4379 + 476 + 58$

2. $1\frac{1}{2}l - 750\,ml$

3. Measure these five lines in mm.

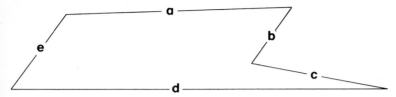

4. Find the average of 460 g, 730 g, 980 g, 370 g and 470 g.

5. $1\frac{3}{5} + 3\frac{1}{2}$

6. $\frac{3}{5} - \frac{1}{4}$

7. Find $\frac{3}{8}$ of £2·64.

8. Calculate the volume of this cuboid.

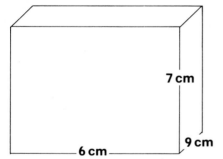

9. Calculate the area of, this shape in m².

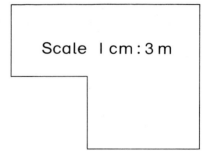

Scale 1 cm : 3 m

10. Make each of these numbers 10 times bigger: 4·3; 64·6; 108·3.

11. $13·4 + 17·8 + 3·9$

12. $15·0 - 7·3$

13. $5·4 \times 6$

14. $6·8 \div 4$

15. Write each of these times in the 24 hour clock way.
4.20 am; 6.55 pm; 3.05 pm.

16. Measure this angle.

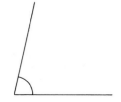

17. £3·87 × 8   **18.** Find $\frac{1}{5}$ of $1\frac{1}{2}$ kg   **19.** Find $\frac{2}{5}$ of 4 metres.

20. Find the average of 3·7, 6·4, 4·3 and 5·2.

21. Draw a graph to show this information.

Number of cards	5	10	15	20	25	30	35
Cost of cards	£1	£2	£3	£4	£5	£6	£7

22. Find the product of 9 and 714.

23. $2\frac{2}{3} + \frac{4}{5}$ **24.** $\frac{5}{6} - \frac{1}{8}$

25. Find the difference between 5 m and 1·76 m.

26. Find $\frac{4}{5}$ of 14 kg.

27. Is this triangle isosceles, equilateral or scalene?

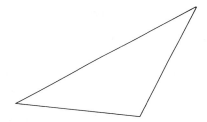

28. The volume is 250 cm³.
What is the width?

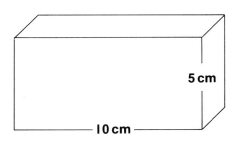

29. The area is 108 m².
What is the length?

30. How many minutes is it from 2105 hrs to 2132 hrs?

Glossary

acute angle — an angle measuring less than 90°

average — the average of 3, 7 and 8 is 6

circumference — the perimeter of a circle

co-ordinate — a pair of numbers that plot position

denominator — the number below the line of the fraction

equilateral triangle — a triangle having three equal sides

isosceles triangle — a triangle having two equal sides

kilometre — a measure of length (1000 m = 1 km)

line graph — a type of graph

millimetre — a measure of length (10 mm = 1 cm)

obtuse angle — an angle less than 180° and more than 90°

product — when two numbers are multiplied together the answer is called the product

protractor — used for measuring angles

radius — the distance from the centre of the circle to the circumference

right angle — a 90° angle

scalene triangle — a triangle having no equal sides

stick graph — a type of graph

straight angle — a 180° angle

volume — the space within a container